FLESH PEDDLERS AND WARM BODIES

THE ARNOLD AND CAROLINE ROSE MONOGRAPH SERIES
OF THE AMERICAN SOCIOLOGICAL ASSOCIATION

FLESH PEDDLERS AND WARM BODIES

The Temporary Help Industry and Its Workers

ROBERT E. PARKER

RUTGERS UNIVERSITY PRESS
New Brunswick, New Jersey

HD
5854.2
.U6
P37
1994

Library of Congress Cataloging-in-Publication Data

Parker, Robert E., 1957–
    Flesh peddlers and warm bodies : the temporary help industry and
its workers / Robert E. Parker.
        p.   cm. — (The Arnold and Caroline Rose monograph series of
the American Sociological Association)
    Includes bibliographical references and index.
    ISBN 0-8135-2036-3 (cloth) — ISBN 0-8135-2089-4 (pbk.)
    1. Temporary employees—United States.   2. Temporary employment—
United States.   I. Title.   II. Series.
HD5854.2.U6P37   1993
331.25'72—dc20   93-24222
                                                                              CIP

British Cataloging-Publication information available

This book is dedicated with all my adoration to Ashley and Chelsea

CONTENTS

LIST OF TABLES

ACKNOWLEDGMENTS

THERE ARE A NUMBER of people I wish to thank for their help and support in preparing this book, particularly the workers and branch managers who were kind and patient enough to engage in often lengthy discussions. I also want to acknowledge W. Norton Grubb, for encouraging me to pursue the topic; Joe R. Feagin, for helping me bring it to fruition as my doctoral dissertation; and Terry A. Sullivan and the Rose Monograph Series staff and board members, for including this book in the series. I also thank the anonymous outside reviewers and Jan Kristiansson, the copyeditor for this project, who took the time to carefully read and criticize the text.

Finally, I want to acknowledge the following individuals for their support during the time this work was in process: Joe R. Feagin, Terry Sullivan, Carollyn Swift, the Derossetts, Rosemary Barone, Robert Zimmerman, Berch Berberoglu, Jim Frey, Veona Hunsinger, Rose Richardson, Denise Carillo, Joan Rozzi, William B. Pike, David Byrne, Mona Thurmond, Neil Young, Mark Gottdiener, Van Morrison, and my parents, Elizabeth and Charles Parker.

FLESH PEDDLERS AND WARM BODIES

1

CONTINGENT WORK AND THE NEW ECONOMY

THE MAJOR FOCUS of this book is to examine critically the emergence and growth of the temporary workforce in the U.S. economy. Temporary workers are a key element in the rapidly advancing "contingent" labor market. Contingent workers, a term originally coined by Conference Board economist Audrey Freedman in the mid-1980s to describe conditional employment arrangements, are now often more broadly conceptualized: as employees with a looser, nontraditional affiliation with their employers. According to a study by Richard Belous, as the 1990s began, between one-quarter and one-third of all employees were a part of the contingent workforce.[1] In addition to the employees of temporary work firms, examples of contingent employment include part-time workers; leased, contracted, or subcontracted workers (usually employed by business service firms); many of the self-employed; multiple job holders; and day laborers.[2] These and similar occupational categories are increasing substantially faster than the U.S. labor force as a whole. Although some workers choose a contingent working status (often for family or other personal reasons), a large and growing percentage of workers are finding contingent positions their only option as the largest corporations in the United States continue to restructure their operations on a worldwide basis.[3]

The Growth of Contingent Work

The contingent workforce is found in both the core (monopoly) and the peripheral sectors of the U.S. economy and is demographically distinct. It is disproportionately composed of the young, the elderly, minorities, and, most frequently, women.[4] The transition to an increasingly contingent workforce provides U.S. businesses with greater flexibility and other benefits but implies several negative effects for workers, including lower wages and the loss of such fringe benefits as health care protection, vacations, pension, and retirement benefits.

Particularly since the early 1980s the marginal or contingent sector of the U.S. labor force has significantly expanded, easily surpassing the overall growth of the U.S. labor force. One study in the late 1980s reported a contingent labor force of between 29.9 million and 36.6 million workers. According to U.S. Bureau of Labor Statistics (BLS) data, the U.S. civilian labor force grew by 14 percent between 1980 and 1988. But during the same period, the number of temporary workers (those specifically recorded as employed by the temporary help services industry) increased by 175 percent, part-time workers (roughly 30 percent of whom work part-time "involuntarily") grew by 21 percent, and the business services industry (which expanded more rapidly during the 1980s than any other industry in the U.S. economy and is the primary provider of subcontracted employees to employers) grew by 70 percent.[5] Traditional economic explanations are not especially useful in understanding this advance since the growth occurred in the midst of one of this country's longest economic expansions. Nonetheless, the role of international economic competition as well as domestic economic changes does offer some insight into this phenomenon. The data suggest a fundamental transformation of the U.S. labor force (a trend documented in other advanced capitalist countries as well).

Indeed, much of the overall employment growth since the mid-1970s has involved the creation of part-time and otherwise impermanent positions. Since the beginning of the 1980s, employers have been aggressively avoiding any long-term commitment to a majority of their workers.[6] Employers are not only pursuing a docile workforce willing to work for low wages and few, if any, benefits; they are also seeking the flexibility to retain workers only for the briefest periods of time when their labor is required. International competition, the restructuring of the domestic economy, and the drive to reduce labor costs are frequently cited by employers as the engines driving their expanding use of contingent workers.

Types of Contingent Workers

Contingent work does not involve one homogeneous type of working arrangement and is not confined to any single economic sector.[7] Nonetheless, several core characteristics tend to be shared by contingent workers. These include low wages; few, if any, fringe benefits; minimal chances for occupational advancement; virtually no opportunity to exert discretion at the workplace; and the inability to utilize existing skills. In addition, many contingent workers have a pervasive sense of uncertainty surrounding their work lives.[8] Given the diversity of temporary occupations in the American workforce, it is clear that the U.S. economy depends upon a large number of workers to fill a variety of jobs on a contingent basis. Employers use temporary, part-time, and other marginal workers in an extensive set of occupational settings. This contingent work force comprises several kinds of workers and work.

Day Laborers

One parallel among day laborers, industrial "temps," part-time employees, and other segments of the contingent workforce is their inability to obtain as much work as they want or, in many cases, require to subsist. Even in rapidly growing cities overwhelmed by construction activity, the supply of work remains inadequate for all those who are actively seeking employment. While sharing this and other features in common, day laborers are far more vulnerable to exploitation and harsh working conditions than are most of the employees of the temporary help industry.

A handful of reports and my field research on day laborers shed further insight into the daily conditions confronted by this type of contingent worker. A study of day laborers by Charles Grigsby in the mid-1980s examined the day labor rituals of five hundred homeless individuals in Austin, Texas.[9] He found that more than 60 percent resorted to "labor corners" to find work. These unregulated labor corners exist in most moderate- to larger-sized cities. Workers congregate at such corners looking for (mainly construction and landscaping) day work, whereas employers gravitate to these areas looking for cheap labor.

In Los Angeles in the early 1990s several thousand laborers, mostly Latino men, gathered each morning seeking work at about twenty-five street corners scattered throughout the city. Interestingly, city officials have been experimenting with programs that will likely institutionalize this type of dead-end, highly exploitative working arrangement. In a plan drawn up in late 1989, day laborers began being bused at city expense to designated day labor centers. Incredibly, a mariachi band played for the workers on the first day of the program, and city workers brought the laborers free coffee and doughnuts. These initiatives are widely seen as stemming from the political pressure exerted on officials from residents who live near the traditional corners.[10] Following Los Angeles's lead, San Francisco is resurrecting hiring halls for the city's day laborers, who now populate street corners in the largely Hispanic Mission District.[11] These newly created (deliberately nonunion) hiring halls are modeled after unionized longshore hiring halls. The intensified use of this type of low-wage nonorganized labor depresses the wages and working conditions for all workers.[12]

As part of my participant-observation research in Austin (I later undertook nonparticipant observation in Las Vegas), I witnessed approximately four hundred individuals (mostly nonwhite males) line up at one street corner (this being just one of several informal, unregulated locations spread across the city) at 5:30 A.M. hunting for day work. By 8:30 most were still jobless, and many were beginning the trek to the state employment office. In all, half the population in this study showed up at labor corners a minimum of twenty times over one documented six-month period.

From the outset, labor corners offer dubious working conditions at best. Day laborers commonly run in front of, alongside of, and into the back of pickup trucks; this is a daily part of their search for work in the two cities where I observed. Seldom are they able to assess what the workday will bring. Homeless and day labor researchers indicate that many of these contingent workers are often underpaid or, worse, are paid in kind in the form of alcohol or cigarettes. And reports of workers sustaining on-the-job injuries without receiving treatment or being dumped at medical facilities are not infrequent. An embellished account of day laborers, including more data from the Grigsby study and my observations, appears in Chapter 3.

Guest Workers

In addition to domestic farm workers and undocumented workers, tens of thousands of "guest workers" (under provisions of the H-2A visa program) perform agricultural work for U.S. employers on a temporary basis. The H-2A visa guest worker program allows American farmers to import workers if they cannot find American employees at the time and place of the harvests. For example, in 1990 Oakley Farms requested nine hundred workers from Mexico to harvest fruit for $.65 per box. In the application process, the grower in effect establishes the working standard; American workers who would work for, say, $.95 per box are not considered eligible. According to the standards of the U.S. Department of Labor's H-2A program, these American workers cannot pick Oakley Farms fruit because they will not work for the grower's mandated wage. The H-2A program also permits about ten thousand workers from Jamaica to temporarily migrate to the United States each year to cut Florida sugar cane.[13] When these migrants have finished their work, they are deported.

Employers of guest workers benefit from their labor in several ways. These employers do not have to pay Social Security, unemployment compensation, or workers' compensation taxes. Furthermore, if the workers complain or cause trouble, employers can quickly have them deported to their native country. Since the early 1980s a steady stream of legislative proposals has called for an expansion of the program to include as many as five hundred thousand guest workers.

According to an early 1980s House Labor Standards Subcommittee report, U.S. farmers prefer to use guest workers even when other workers are available. For instance, in the 1980s thousands of immigrants arrived from Cuba, Haiti, and other Caribbean nations. In addition, hundreds of thousands more have arrived from Central America. The majority of these immigrants are unskilled and often are from rural areas; seemingly they could provide all the cheap labor farm operators would demand.

Yet the House report clearly indicated that Florida farm operators have consistently requested workers from among the poorest British West Indian applicants. Clearly, employers see these workers as the most willing to work long, hard hours without complaining about conditions and to constitute a workforce that is cheap, compliant, and apolitical. The House report concluded, "Foreign guest workers who survive the rigors of a six-day week, five month harvest season provide the growers with an elite corps of experienced sugar cane cutters that cannot strike, organize, or effectively protest."[14]

(Business) Service Workers

For several decades service occupations have grown faster than other segments of the U.S. labor force. As defined by the Bureau of Labor Statistics in 1991, there were sixteen million workers employed in service occupations, including health service workers, cleaning workers, and private household workers. As with other elements of the contingent workforce, these jobs are disproportionately filled by women (61 percent of the total). And like other industries in the U.S. economy, part-time workers make up a growing part of the service sector. Between 1979 and the mid-1980s, the percentage of part-time workers within the service sector escalated more sharply than any other set of industries from 17.8 percent to 31.1 percent. This gain of more than 13 percentage points in part-time work in the service industries dwarfed that of most others, including transportation (+0.7), manufacturing (+2.6), construction (+2.9), wholesale trade (+4.9), and retail trade (+5.5). Furthermore, service industries, which

Table 1.1 Contingent and Total Civilian Workforce Growth, 1980–1991

	Number of workers		
	1980	*1991*	*Percent change*
Temporary workers	0.4	1.3*	225.0
Business service workers	3.3	6.18	87.3
Part-time workers	16.3	20.3	24.5
Self-employed	8.5	10.3	21.2
Total labor force	106.9	125.3	17.2

Source: Adapted from Richard Belous, *The Contingent Economy: The Growth of the Temporary, Part-Time,and Subcontracted Workforce* (Washington, D.C.: National Planning Association, 1989), p. 16.
These data are not directly comparable to data before 1990, when "leased employees" were added to SIC 7363 (Help Supply Services).

are eclectic in composition, employ 40.5 percent of all part-time workers.[15] Of the sixteen million service workers in 1991, for example, more than two million were "protective service" workers, while roughly five million were food preparation and service workers.

These figures illustrate the arbitrariness of official definitions of occupations. Consider the tens of thousands of other service workers in the U.S. economy—some well paid with high occupational status. In 1991, for example, there were thirty-one million "managers" and professional workers listed outside the ranks of "service" occupations. But the most rapidly growing "service" jobs are low-wage, dead-end positions typical of other occupations in the contingent category. Except for temporary workers, no segment of the contingent workforce has been growing as rapidly as employees of business services (see Table 1.1). Despite the rapid growth of the business services industry, its significance has received little sustained attention.

The business services industry is the main provider of subcontracted labor, which in itself is a growing part of the contingent workforce. Key sectors within this industry include computer and data processing services; advertising; consumer credit reporting and collection; mailing, reproduction, and stenographic services; building services; and personnel services. Workers in this industry are disassociated from the traditional employer-employee relationship. They are less likely to be unionized, have a job tenure average half that of the national median, and generally receive lower pay and fewer benefits.

Temporary Clerical Workers

Between 1940 and the beginning of the 1990s, the number of clerical jobs in the U.S. economy increased from 4.4 million to nearly 20 million.[16] This burgeoning white-collar workforce has become central to the emergence and expansion of the new contingent economy. For example, clerical workers are the single most frequent type of worker dispatched by temporary help firms to employers. As has been true for more than a decade, in 1990 approximately 65 percent of all temporary help assignments were for clerical positions.[17] Even though other occupational categories within the temporary industry are accelerating at a faster pace (such as temporary home health care workers), clerical positions continue to provide the greatest number of employment opportunities for temporary workers. Clerk-typists, secretaries, file and data-entry clerks, bookkeepers, and receptionists account for the bulk of the clerical occupations. Like involuntary part-time workers, temporary clerical workers express a preference for full-time, year-round employment, but eventually most are forced to accept whatever work they can find.

Consistent with the composition of other components of the contingent workforce, the vast majority of these workers are female. Prior to the Civil War, most clerical workers were male. But by 1988, 80 percent of clerical employees were women.[18] And a recent worker survey conducted by the National Association of Temporary Services (NATS) showed that 80 percent of all respondents were female.[19]

Among the growing ranks of contingent clerical workers, many have arrived at their marginal status through similar circumstances. For example, a sizable number, perhaps a majority, of the most recent members are victims of U.S. corporate restructuring. As companies "rationalize" and "downsize," they are creating virtually captive pools of talented labor that business services, subcontractors, temporary help companies, and other employers can exploit.[20] Some clerical workers are recent arrivals in an urban area and, unable to locate permanent, full-time employment, turn to a temporary, contingent arrangement. Still others are trying to enter the labor market on a full-time basis for the first time and cannot find full-time work. Finally, some contingent workers are accustomed to full-time positions but are in between jobs because of resignations, terminations, and other types of layoffs.

Temporary Industrial Workers

Like most contingent workers, temporary industrial workers tend to be full-time job seekers. And like involuntary part-time workers, subcontractors, and others in the marginalized workforce, industrial workers employed by the temporary help industry are an underemployed segment of the labor force. They endure uncertain hours, inadequate income, and a fundamental mismatch between their existing skills and the working opportunities offered by the temporary help industry. According to Steven Wasser, temporary industrial workers account for a little more than 7 percent of total temporary help industry revenues and 9 percent of total employment.[21] According to more recent estimates by Office Specialists (a temporary help firm), between 1986 and 1989 industrial workers within the temporary help industry declined from 16 percent to a little less than 15 percent.[22]

Temporary industrial employees are typically requested by companies to perform warehouse or some other type of "mindless" manual work. Other common assignments include laboring positions such as construction, light assembly and manufacturing, physical plant maintenance, and inventory work. The majority of work assigned to temporary industrial workers requires few, if any, skills. The only prerequisite is a willingness to follow directions and to perform physically demanding labor. With the exception of electronics assembly workers (who must know how to solder), most temporary work assignments involve the use of unskilled labor.

Like many other segments of the contingent workforce, many temporary industrial workers have marketable skills and have previously held full-time positions. Yet in the early 1990s, they could not find full-time, year-round, permanent jobs. Temporary industrial workers frequently report having full-time working experience in areas such as construction work, maintenance, electronics assembly, transportation, and saleswork. And like other parts of the contingent army of the underemployed, most arrive at temporary work only after exhausting other, more preferable alternatives.

Part-Time Workers

Another type of contingent work that has minimized employers' labor costs and increased profits is part-time employment. The number of part-time workers and their percentage in the labor force have been growing rapidly since the 1970s, particularly among women.[23] As noted earlier, from 1980 to the early 1990s the number of part-time workers in the U.S. labor force advanced much more rapidly than the total labor force. Noting the rapid rise in part-time work, Susan McHenry and Linda Lee Small observed that more than 25 percent of the "much heralded 10 million jobs created during the Reagan era were part-time."[24]

The expansion of part-time work continued through nearly eight years of economic expansion into a new decade. As Chris Tilly recently summed, "Part-time employees comprise almost one-fifth of the U.S. work force. About 20 million people in the economy's non-agricultural sectors worked part time in 1989, making up 18.1 percent of persons at work. . . . Since the late 1950s, the fraction of those at work consisting of part-timers has grown gradually, rising from 12.1 percent in 1957 to its current 18 percent."[25]

Moreover, relying on official statistics can be misleading. Tilly noted that the increase in part-time employment would appear even more severe if Department of Labor and Census Bureau statisticians counted the number of part-time jobs rather than the number of part-time workers. A record number of workers in the early 1990s, for instance, held multiple jobs. Although counted as full-time workers because they worked more than 35 hours per week, in terms of pay, benefits, and other working conditions this group of workers more closely resembled involuntary part-time workers.

Involuntary Part-Time Workers

Another category of employees attracting increasing attention and concern is involuntary part-time workers. As the BLS counts them, these workers take part-time jobs out of economic necessity (they are the only jobs workers can find, or a worker's usual full-time job becomes part-time temporarily or permanently). Much of the recent increase in part-time employment is attributable to the rise in the number of involuntary part-time workers. For example, between 1970 and 1982, when the number of voluntary part-time workers rose from 9.3 million to 12.4 million (a 33 percent increase), the number of involuntary part-time workers grew by 166 percent, from 2.19 million to 5.8 million employees.[26] After this very rapid period of growth during the 1970s and the 1980–1982 recessionary period, the growth rate among part-time workers slowed somewhat. However, increases among involuntary part-time workers have continued, and overall levels remain stubbornly high, particularly given the sustained economic expansion of the 1980s.

The trend toward higher levels of involuntary part-time work was demonstrable in the early 1990s as the business cycle entered another recessionary phase. Despite the slower growth increase in the 1980s, between 1970 and 1990 the involuntary part-time workforce still advanced by 121 percent, compared with 69 percent for voluntary part-time workers and 54 percent for all workers. Recent data from the Department of Labor showed 5.7 million involuntary part-time workers in the labor force in mid-1991, one million more than the figure recorded a year earlier. On average, the involuntary part-time workforce has been increasing more than twice as rapidly as the civilian labor force since the early 1970s.[27]

Creative bookkeeping by employers also cautions us to be critical of official statistics on part-time workers. Consider the accounting practices of a company like Giant Eagle (the only supermarket chain in Pittsburgh and an extensive employer of part-time employees). In the mid-1980s, of Giant Eagle's more than six thousand workers, 80 percent were part-time. These workers were paid a lower hourly rate than full-time employees and received fewer fringe benefits. At the same time the company hired workers who were part time in name only; these workers routinely labored longer than the thirty-five hours designated as part-time by the BLS. Yet unlike full-time workers, they did not receive similar wages or benefits.[28]

The calculated, planned use of contingent workers began in earnest following the recessions of the 1970s and 1980s. The growing severity and increasing rapidity with which recessions occurred during this period made employers in many industries particularly sensitive to production costs, especially labor-related ones. For the managers of many large organizations, the fastest and easiest way to reduce costs is to dismiss workers. With the recession of the early 1990s and other contractions still fresh in their memories, employers are reluctant to hire full-time, year-round, permanent workers.

Temporary Workers

Having briefly illustrated other elements of the increasingly prominent contingent workforce, I wish to highlight some of the more salient aspects of temporary work life. Although many types of temporary workers exist in the U.S. labor force, this book is largely concerned with the employees of temporary help firms such as Manpower, Inc. and Kelly Services.[29] Other types of temporary workers will be discussed in greater detail later to more fully illuminate the working conditions faced by the employees of the more established temporary help industry.

There have been several studies of temporary help firms and their clients.[30] These efforts, however, are largely in the tradition of industrial organization studies, concentrating on the operation of temporary help firms and their clients while generally neglecting the perspective of the temporary worker. As Garth Mangum, Donald Mayall, and Kristin Nelson observed, "An obvious limitation of our analysis is that we have investigated only the employer's attitudes and responses to temporary work needs. A parallel study of the supply side—the temporary worker—is obviously necessary to complement our conclusions."[31]

There have been some notable efforts to draw attention to the worker's vantage point in the rapidly expanding contingent economy.[32] But by and large these studies have been brief and have lacked a thoroughgoing firsthand account of what it means to be a temporary worker. There have also been few attempts to ground the transformation toward a contingent economy with concrete examples, even though the data are becoming more familiar as more workers experience contingent employment and the issue is more widely discussed. An attempt to convey a sense of what it means to be a temporary worker employed by a highly rationalized industry is also needed and filling that gap is at the center of this book.

Temporary employment is worthy of sustained scholarly attention even without the reasons outlined here. The temporary help industry's economic impact is significant in today's service-oriented economy. The revenue garnered by temporary help companies between 1985 and 1989 advanced from $11.2 billion to nearly $19 billion (in constant 1985 dollars).[33] In addition, the industry's workforce is growing rapidly and becoming less sensitive to cyclical variations. Between 1982 and 1990 temporary and leased employment increased from a little more than 400,000 workers to nearly 1.3 million.[34]

Studies of Underemployment

From the employees' vantage point, temporary work can accurately be characterized as a new form of underemployment. The employees of the temporary help industry are mainly full-time job seekers who earn lower wages, receive fewer fringe benefits than full-time workers, and more easily fall through the tears in the country's social safety net. Temporary workers must also endure uncertain working hours and a lack of opportunities to utilize skills.

One outcome of being understudied is that temporary employment has been all but entirely neglected as a new form of labor market hardship. The U.S. economy since the 1970s has created many forms of distress among American workers. Despite a declining unemployment rate during most of that time, high levels of discouraged, involuntary, part-time, displaced, low-wage, and moonlighting workers persisted.

Yet with few exceptions, existing studies of labor market hardship omit temporary workers and their role in the economy.[35] For example, although the number of unemployed workers has declined from the post–World War II peak reached in 1982, there were approximately twenty-one million workers who experienced unemployment at some time during 1985 and more than fourteen million full-time workers who had to work part time for at least part of the year. As Sar Levitan and Isaac Shapiro's *Working But Poor* and a series of reports by the BLS made clear, labor market hardship is of great import.[36] For example, among the twenty-one million workers who were unemployed at some point in 1985, 21.4 percent lived in families below the poverty line, a level that was nearly twice as high as the national average. The number of workers with low earnings also remained high through the 1980s. In 1985 more than four million employees worked year round and full time but still earned less than someone working year round at minimum wage. Among these workers a little more than 31 percent lived in families below the poverty line.

Involuntary part-time workers also experience employment hardship. Between 1970 and 1982, when employment overall grew by nearly 27 percent, the number of part-time workers expanded by 58 percent. But this rapid rise was dwarfed by the 166 percent gain posted for the number of involuntary part-time workers during the same period. Deborah Wise, Aaron Bernstein and Alice Cuneo expressed the expansion of involuntary part-time workers in the economy this way: in 1976 involuntary part-time workers accounted for 4.1 percent of the labor force, compared with 5.5 percent in 1984.[37] Approximately 10.2 million employees worked part time involuntarily for at least twenty-seven weeks in 1987. Approximately 20 percent of these workers lived in households below the officially defined poverty threshold.[38]

In a series of reports, the BLS documented the increasingly close connection among poverty and low-wage work, involuntary part-time employment, and those who experience intermittent unemployment.[39] These and other categories of underemployment have received at least cursory attention, but temporary work has yet to be formally addressed as a unique type of marginal employment.[40] Yet temporary workers are for the most part just that, marginalized members of the labor force. Generally, they are full-time job seekers who apply for temporary assignments because such employment is the only work available.

Among the workers I interviewed, except for those who had full-time positions to which to return (such as schoolteachers), all wanted full-time employment. Other writers covering temporary workers have also intimated that full-time employment is the first choice among this group of workers.[41] Finally, temporary workers represent an underemployed pool of employees in that their compensation is approximately one-third of that received by full-time employees. By these and other criteria, temporary workers should be incorporated into contemporary studies of underemployment.

A small group of scholarly observers have recognized that labor force statistics distort and typically understate the magnitude of employment problems in the U.S. labor market. One early effort to determine the extent of underemployment was initiated by Secretary of Labor W. Willard Wirtz in 1966. Wirtz's "subemployment" measure included those officially defined as unemployed: involuntary part-time workers, family heads with full-time jobs who were earning less than enough to raise a family of four above the poverty threshold, individuals who were earning less than the minimum-wage equivalent in full-time jobs, half of all males aged twenty to sixty-four who were not in the labor force (a proxy measure for discouragement), and an adjustment for the census undercount. When this measure was applied in eight major cities, the Department of Labor calculated that 34.7 percent of the adult population was subemployed.[42]

Confronted with conservative criticism that the new labor market measure had been used as a "scare index" to gain support for Great Society social programs, the Department of Labor published a national subemployment rate in the 1968 *Manpower Report of the President.* This index was more restrictive in conceptualizing subemployment. It included all full-time workers earning less than a poverty-level income and those unemployed fifteen or more weeks during the year. By this measure, "a tenth of the labor force was subemployed in 1966, a decline from 17 percent in 1961."[43]

In 1972, the research of social scientists exploring new theoretical paradigms, including "segmented labor market" theory and "dual labor market theory," gave rise to the development of a new underemployment index. This research, done for the Census Bureau and covering fifty-one large cities, was largely ignored by the Nixon administration's politically unsympathetic Department of Labor. However, the Senate Subcommittee on Employment, Manpower, and Poverty showed greater interest, publishing the data in 1972. The results of the study were also translated into an index and published by William Spring, Bennett Harrison, and Thomas Vietorisz.[44] Their index, which found an overall subemployment rate of nearly 31 percent, included the officially defined unemployed, involuntary part-time workers, discouraged workers, and full-time low-wage earners.

Like earlier efforts, this report received a chilly political reception. Critics held that low-wage workers should have been counted only if they were heads of households since a low-wage teenager did not automatically imply family hardship. To address this criticism, Herman Miller developed an index with a more restrictive set of categories.[45] With the same census data used by Spring and his associates, Miller applied his index to the nation's twelve largest cities. Although this measure excluded workers aged sixteen to twenty-one, those older than sixty-five, and all persons with above-average incomes, it still registered a 19.4 percent subemployment figure in 1970.[46]

In addition to these indices, other attempts to assess the magnitude of underemployment have been pursued; most typically include some combination of the unemployed, low-wage workers, and those working on a part-time basis involuntarily. Sar Levitan and Robert Taggart, for example, designed the Employment and Earnings Inadequacy Index to measure the number of "persons who experience difficulties in competing for gainful employment paying an adequate wage."[47] Their operational criteria were similar to those used in Miller's index. Using data from the 1972 March Current Population Survey, these two researchers calculated a 14.9 percent subemployment level. Another index, developed by Thomas Vietorisz, Robert Mier, and Jean-Ellen Giblin, attempted to measure "the extent to which the labor market does not provide the needed number of adequate jobs."[48] Using the 1970 Detroit Census Employment Survey, these researchers found subemployment among half the workers in Detroit.

Philip M. Hauser's development of a "labor utilization framework" is another attempt to gauge levels of underemployment.[49] It is the only measure that uses the entire labor force as its target population. Unlike other indices of hardship, it excludes discouraged workers but adds the mismatch between occupation and skill level as a dimension of underemployment. In Teresa Sullivan's application of the Labor Utilization Framework, she found adequate working hours more widespread than adequate income and adequate income more common than the use of advanced skill levels. Her empirical analysis revealed that underutilization declined from 25.1 percent in 1960 to 23.3 percent in 1970.[50]

Temporary Work as a New Form of Underemployment

This brief review of efforts to gauge the extent of underemployment in U.S. labor markets demonstrates the neglect of temporary workers. Nor do existing studies include day laborers, contract workers, limited-duration hires, the enormous number of temporary workers in the federal government, or the one-quarter (or more) of all college instructors nationwide who work on a part-time schedule. Because of this omission in the literature, the rapid emergence and expansion of temporary employment are clearly deserving of scholarly attention.

Although some workers choose temporary schedules, the available evidence suggests that most temporary workers are searching for full-time, permanent employment. Even those temporary employees who told me they were generally assigned a sufficient amount of work often did not consistently receive adequate hours on a weekly basis. Clearly, temps share much in common with involuntary part-time workers. Even temporary workers who are steadily employed appear disadvantaged compared with other types of contingent workers. As Mayall and Nelson noted, "Employees of temporary help companies generally receive considerably less in terms of benefits than permanent workers in the same line of work, or even temporary workers covered by collective bargaining agreements. . . . Virtually none provide for accrual of retirement benefits, which are commonly part of union benefit packages, even for temporary workers."[51]

Finally, in the area of skill utilization, it is clear that temporary employees warrant classification as part of the underemployed. Typically, temps are assigned to the least interesting and least challenging positions within the organizations to which they are assigned. And temporary employees are disproportionately represented in dull, dirty jobs with high turnover rates. Primary and secondary empirical accounts strongly suggest that temporary work is a new and growing variant of underemployment and should be recognized as such, along with other contingent components of the workforce. In contrast to the industry's public-relations portrayal of temporary employees as unskilled, newly arriving entrants to the workforce; housewives filled with trepidation about labor force reentry; and youthful pleasure seekers, most temporary workers are simply searching for full-time jobs. Generally, they work on a temporary basis because other working opportunities are unavailable.

Public and Private Uses of Temporary Workers

The expansion of temporary employment has important public and private policy implications. By examining the uses and users of temporary employees, we can gauge the potential impact this growing industry will have on the U.S. economy and larger society.

For the private sector, temporary employees are a critical part of the corporate quest for a flexible workforce. By increasing the use of temporary employees, employers can maintain a smaller (even minimum) number of permanent workers on their payrolls. Encouraged by the temporary services industry, employers are extensively adopting this type of "planned staffing" strategy.

But private employers are not the only actors keeping the temporary help industry growing and prosperous. Temporary workers are now being used in far greater numbers in the public sector. This trend was accelerated (in a major policy switch) by the director of the Office of Personnel Management (OPM), Donald Devine. In 1985 in a key directive, he gave all federal agencies broad new authority to hire and retain temporary employees without going through the competitive selection process required for permanent civil service appointments. The year before this directive there were nearly 245,000 temporary appointments in a 2.2 million federal employee workforce.[52]

Not only is this switch problematic for the workers involved; it also raises questions about human resource policy in the public sector. Employing large numbers of workers with an explicitly temporary attachment to public service may serve to undermine the delivery of government services. Consider that many thousands of temps are hired annually to work in essential agencies such as the Internal Revenue Service (IRS) and the Postal Service.

This book, then, while drawing attention to the advent of the temporary help industry and to other types of contingent workers, fundamentally concentrates on temporary employment from the worker's point of view. From this perspective the dire implications of this new form of underemployment for the U.S. labor force become clear. The chapters that follow examine the temporary help industry and provide an inside look at what it means to be employed as a temp worker in today's economy. Furthermore, this book locates the emergence and spread of temporary employment in a broader social context, particularly the unrelenting corporate demand for a flexible workforce.

Methodological Approach

An eclectic methodological approach was central in researching this topic, particularly the use of in-depth interviews with key informants, a period of ethnographic fieldwork, and an examination of popular, professional, and industrial literature. Over a five-month period, I completed eleven in-depth interviews with branch managers of temporary help firms. These interviews with the managers took an average of two hours to complete. Of the eleven branch managers, seven were women.

Their tenure as branch manager varied considerably. For example, one branch manager had held her executive post for twenty-two years, whereas another manager had finished working as a receptionist just three weeks before our interview. Only two had previous experience in the "personnel supply industry" before arriving at their present position. They were also diverse in terms of formal educational attainment. Most, eight of eleven, had at least a bachelor's degree, with business and communications being the two most common fields. Of the remaining three managers, two had a master's degree. The diversity of their backgrounds also extended to previous occupations, with middle-level management being one common category. In all, the branch managers responded to nearly fifty questions covering three central areas: employee working conditions, the organization and structure of the temporary help industry, and the functions that temporary employment serves for public and private employers (see Appendix).

Over a six-month period I was able to arrange forty-one in-depth interviews with employees of the temporary help industry. The forty-one were "screened" from a larger pool of approximately one hundred workers with whom I associated and from whom I gathered significant, but not complete information. The respondents included twenty clerical and twenty light industrial workers. The remaining interview was with a home health care worker employed by a provider of temporary health services. Among the temporary industrial workers, eighteen were male. Among the clerical workers, eighteen were female.

As with the branch managers, demographic diversity characterized the temporary workers who participated in this study. Among clerical workers, the average age was twenty-seven and one-half, with the range from eighteen to forty-seven years. All the twenty clerical workers had at least completed high school. Three had completed a bachelor's degree, and one had earned a master's degree. Among the twenty clerical employees, seventeen had completed at least some college. With one exception—a Hispanic female—all the clerical workers were white.

Among the industrial temps, the age distribution (twenty-two to fifty-one) was similar, but these workers had completed less formal education. Among the twenty, one had failed to complete high school, nine had achieved high school diplomas, six had completed some college, two had a bachelor's degree, one had a master's degree, and one had completed a formal technical training program. Nonwhites were disproportionately represented among the industrial workers. Half the industrial workers interviewed were minority members: eight African Americans, one Latino, and one Asian American.

There was a bimodal distribution among both clerical and industrial workers with respect to their tenure as an employee of a temporary help firm. Six clerical and seven industrial workers had been employed as a temp for one month or less. Seven industrial workers and five clerical workers had been working as a temp for one year or more. A majority of the remainder had been temping for nine months or less. Both clerical and industrial workers responded to thirty in-depth questions covering major aspects of their experience as temporary employees (see Appendix).

I gleaned additional information about the temporary help industry and its workers from interactions with workers and temporary service personnel during my four-month stint as an employee of the temporary help industry. Becoming a temporary worker is not difficult. During this period I applied for work and was employed by three different temporary help firms. Once employed, I stayed active by keeping myself available for whatever kinds of assignments were offered. I maintained regular interaction by phone and periodic visits to temporary help offices. The participant-observation aspect of this project was key. It provided me with access to other temporary workers and with many firsthand experiences that permitted a fuller understanding of this industry and its workers.

Many scholars have noted methodological problems associated with participant-observation research. In anticipation of the most common, I extended my qualitative effort by gathering data from other materials, from temporary help firms, and from state and national temporary industry associations. Finally, I collected and examined academic, popular, business, and industry literature.

2

THE TEMPORARY HELP INDUSTRY

TEMPORARY HELP SUPPLY companies are private businesses that recruit workers to perform a variety of job tasks and then sell these workers' labor for a set fee. Temporary help companies are employers; they are not, for example, employment agencies. Temporary help firms are businesses that recruit, screen, and dispatch workers, receiving privately controlled revenue in return. These firms are not primarily in the business of helping the unemployed find jobs. Rather, they lend their ever-rotating pool of employees to other organizations for a profit.

This fee-for-labor identity has been deliberately distorted, largely because of the public-relations efforts of the temporary help industry. In a background paper the National Association of Temporary Services claimed that "the temporary help industry is fundamentally a labor market intermediary. It helps facilitate the movement of potential workers into the workforce and into positions of productivity. Because of this, it helps make the labor market function better to the benefit of workers and employers alike."[1] Industry leaders have echoed this definition of temporary firms as labor market intermediaries. While acknowledging that temporary firms are leasing their own employees, Manpower, Inc.'s chief executive officer (CEO), Mitchell Fromstein, claimed that workers and clients treat the temporary firm practically and functionally as an intermediary. Fromstein maintained that "the most prominent and widely applied socioeconomic role of the temporary help industry is that of facilitating the re-entry of workers, especially women, after a long absence from

23

the workforce." Furthermore, he asserted that firms such as Manpower have "offered one of the most effective result records to date in relieving at least a portion of the problem" of youth unemployment. In his less than critical analysis, Fromstein conveniently ignored the many "socioeconomic roles" the temporary help industry creates for itself (profits) and for its customers (a flexible, low-wage, nonunion, easily controlled workforce).[2]

Sar Levitan, Garth Mangum, and Ray Marshall provided another example of the tendency to identify temporary help firms primarily in terms of their intermediary function.[3] In their book *Human Resources and Labor Markets*, Levitan and his co-authors observed that the temporary help company lies somewhere between limited access and publicly accessible labor market intermediaries. Despite an academic perspective (and seemingly detached orientation), the authors' evaluation was hardly more probing or critical than Fromstein's when they concluded, "All in all, the temporary help phenomenon seems to be a good example of enterprise and adaptability with employer and employee need satisfactorily merged."[4]

Although in some ways technically correct, these descriptions of temporary help companies are nevertheless misleading. The labor market intermediary role is clearly a secondary concern for such establishments. Temporary firms are fundamentally private-sector enterprises organized, justified, and driven by the profit-maximization goal they share with other private businesses. The suggestion that temporary companies exist mainly to serve the needs of workers—whether they are workforce reentrants or hard-core unemployed youth—appears disingenuous and inconsistent with the ethnographic research findings underlying this account of temporary work, including the testimony offered by managers of temporary help firms and temporary employees.

Their firsthand descriptions clearly create the impression that temporary help firms are first and foremost employers and that only in a tangential sense can they be considered labor market intermediaries supplying mutual assistance to employers and workers alike. Indeed, temporary help companies actually inhibit workers from making the transition from the temporary to the permanent workforce by charging "liquidated damages" to employers that hire these workers.

The legal status of temporary help firms as employers was established by the U.S. Treasury. In a 1951 ruling, the commissioner of the IRS held that for purposes of federal employment tax and income tax withholding, "you [Employers Overload] are the employer of the employees furnished to these concerns" that request temporary or occasional assistance.[5] Since this ruling temporary help firms have been legally obligated to act as employers. This means, for example, that temporary companies are required to issue payroll checks, deduct and pay federal and state taxes, contribute to the employer portion of the Social Security system, provide workers' compensation, and pay unemployment insurance premiums.

Temporary help companies, then, are principally private-sector businesses whose main objectives are profitability and expansion. As previously intimated, managers of temporary help firms indicate that actively assisting workers is a peripheral concern. Furthermore, the industry avoids discussing the working conditions it offers to workers as an employer. The "labor market intermediary" is an effective label for cloaking the more central business concerns of expansion, increasing sales, and higher profits. When projected as labor market intermediaries, temporary help companies can evoke imagery of beneficent firms with little concern for private profits. Through the heavy use of public relations, including the couching of industry activity in pseudo-scientific human resource terminology, temporary firms can appear as neutral, even altruistic organizations dedicated eto helping workers struggle through hard times in a tight labor market.

Blurring the lines between themselves and public-sector intermediaries, such as public employment agencies, allows temporary help firms to divert attention from their own generally dubious record as employers. Temporary help firm recruits do not enjoy high wages, access to generous fringe benefits, or pleasant (or even consistent) working environments. Thus the industry emphasizes its alleged intermediary role. Despite this rather blatant effort to beguile employees and the public about the industry's primary economic and organizational objectives, temporary help companies are in business for private economic gain. As such, they need to be evaluated primarily in terms of their record as employers, not in terms of a secondary role they also happen to fulfill occasionally.

Industry Growth

Payroll Growth

As measured by several key barometers, the temporary help services industry has recently been one of the most rapidly growing sectors of the U.S. economy. In 1970 the industry had an annual payroll of $547 million. This figure had increased to more than $3 billion a decade later, hit $14 billion in 1991, and exceeded $16 billion in 1992 (see Table 2.1).[6] Between 1970 and 1981, despite three recessions, the industry experienced an annual average payroll growth rate of 19 percent.[7]

Over time, employment and other economic barometers of the temporary help industry have grown less sensitive to changes in the business cycle.[8] This "secular" growth portends industry growth faster than average for the foreseeable future. As Wasser noted, temporary help merits the "'growth industry' label. Not only has it grown nearly twice as fast as GNP over the past 14 years, it has also grown faster than the highly touted computer industry (7.5% vs. 6.2% during 1970–83)."[9]

During the two recessions of the early and mid-1970s, the industry as measured by payroll dropped faster and further than the overall gross national product (GNP). During the recession of the early 1980s, the change was not as dramatic, as the industry closely paralleled the performance of the GNP. According to Wasser, the relative strength of the industry during recent recessions was attributable to its rapidly growing technical segment.[10]

Conversely, in the 1970s and 1980s the industry generally grew five times faster than the GNP when the economy was in an expansionary phase. Between 1970 and 1984 the temporary help industry grew (using unadjusted data) at an annual rate of more than 18 percent. During the same time GNP grew just 9.5 percent. The remaining years of the 1980s proved to be lucrative ones for the temporary help industry, again providing evidence of how the industry has managed to insulate itself from larger economic cycles. According to data calculated by Heidi Hartmann and June Lapidus, in constant 1982 dollars temporary industry payroll grew at a rate of 754 percent in the 1970s and 236 percent in the 1980s.[11] Other sources have also

Table 2.1 Temporary Help Industry Annual Payroll,
           Selected Years

Year	Payroll (million)	Percent change
1970	547.4	—
1980	3,117.2	470
1985	6,375.6	104
1991	13,945.0	120
1992	16,750.0	19

Sources: 1970–1985 data from Bob Whalen and Susan Dennis, "The Temporary Help Industry: An Annual Update," p. 4, reprint from *Contemporary Times* (Spring 1991); 1991 data from "Temp Workers in 1991 Earned $14 Billion," *Christian Science Monitor,* December 18, 1992; 1992 data from telephone interview with Bruce Steinberg, NATS spokesperson, November 19, 1993.

reported rapid growth. Census data in *Current Business Reports* showed that the receipts of temporary help service firms nearly doubled between 1985 and 1989. Measured in constant 1985 dollars, receipts advanced from $11.2 billion to $18.8 billion.[12] Such rapid growth in an economic sector and its social effects deserves heightened scrutiny.

Employment Growth

In addition to the increase in payroll growth, data on employment growth further document this expanding industry. According to the U.S. Department of Commerce's *1985 U.S. Industrial Outlook,* "The largest contributors to employment [between 1981 and 1984] were eating and drinking services, personnel supply services, grocery stores and computer and data processing services."[13] Between 1982 and 1984 the number of workers employed by the temporary help industry rose by 70 percent, making it the *fastest*-growing industry in the U.S. economy (among industries with fifty thousand or more workers). The number of workers in the industry grew by an annual average of more than 7 percent between 1970 and 1981. Between 1976 and 1980 the average annual growth rate was even higher—15.5 percent.

Contrary to the pattern found during previous business cycles, employment growth in the industry did not stop with the end of the recession in the early 1980s (see Table 2.2). According to data published by the Department of Labor in February 1993, there were 1,727,600 employees working for personnel supply services. Of these, 1,493,600 were employed by Help Supply Services.[14]

An important source of data on temporary workers between 1982 and 1989 was the BLS's Standard Industrial Code (SIC) 7362, a subheading under Personnel Services (SIC 73). This code tracked the employees of temporary help firms and the temporary workers they sent on assignments. As of 1990, however, the 7362 code was eliminated and combined with SIC 7363, which is Help Supply Services. The Help Supply Services code includes leased employees and miscellaneous personnel services. Thus, this new category will not be comparable across decades. For the period between 1982 and 1990, employment in Help Supply Services grew from 417,200 workers to 1,295,900.[15] Despite the combining of these categories, the number of workers tracked by the BLS is close to the more narrowly defined category recorded by private sources. According to NATS, there were approximately 1.35 million workers employed by the temporary help industry in 1992.[16] Officially, even with this growth the number of temporary workers in the labor force is small (in 1992 about 1.2 percent of the civilian nonagricultural workforce).

Industry and government-supplied data must not be accepted uncritically. For example, the data on workers are annual averages. The number of people who work as temporary employees at some time during the year is much higher. During 1989, when a little more than 1 million workers were employed by the industry on an average annualized basis, 6.5 million employees worked for a temporary firm at some point during the year.[17] Moreover, these data cover just those employees working for temporary help firms and leave out, for example, the hundreds of thousands of temporary workers employed by the federal government (including the aforementioned postal workers and IRS employees). The data also neglect direct hires—temporary employees who work directly for a business.

Table 2.2 Help Supply Services (SIC 7363) Employment, 1970–1993

Year	Number of employees (average)	Percent change
1993	1,493,600*	4.7
1992	1,426,500	12.5
1990	1,295,900	25.5
1989	1,031,500	−1.1
1988	1,042,600	9.9
1987	948,400	17.4
1986	807,600	14.0
1985	708,200	13.8
1984	622,400	31.9
1983	471,800	16.0
1982	417,200	1.3
1981	401,361	−3.5
1980	416,071	−4.7
1979	436,445	25.3
1978	348,169	18.6
1977	293,728	25.9
1976	233,322	25.0
1975	186,600	−25.5
1974	250,636	23.0
1973	203,706	23.8
1972	164,550	9.3
1971	150,573	−18.3
1970	184,400	−

Sources: U.S. Department of Labor, Bureau of Labor Statistics, *Employment and Earnings* (Washington, D.C.: GPO, various years); U.S. Department of Labor, *Employment Hours, and Earnings, United States, 1981–93*, Bureau of Labor Statistics Bulletin 2429 (Washington, D.C.: GPO, 1993), p. 431.
*As of February 1993.

Using in-house temps or direct hires on a temporary basis has become a central component in the reorganized staffing patterns of many private enterprises, including Control Data Corporation, Travelers Insurance, and Cigna Insurance.[18] Public-sector employers such as educational institutions as well as nonprofit organizations frequently use in-house temporary workers. And, significantly, the official data on temporary workers omit the millions of other workers who can be classified as contingent employees. In any event, it is difficult to accurately track the number of temporary employees because (according to industry spokespersons) the industry's annual turnover rate is between 600 and 700 percent. Confounding matters further is the fact that the average employee only works for a given temporary help company for five to six weeks.

Office Expansion and Industry Concentration

Coinciding with employment and payroll growth is a steady increase in the number of temporary help companies. In 1993, there were more than 2,400 temporary help supply companies operating approximately 16,000 offices in the United States.[19] Between 1975 and 1980 the number of firms grew from 3,133 to 5,178, or by 65 percent. In 1963 there had been just 820 offices nationwide.

Within this expansionary environment, not all temporary help companies have been advancing at the same rate. Proportionately, the mid- to larger-sized temporary offices are experiencing the most rapid growth. Large operators, such as Manpower, Inc. and Kelly Services, are growing more rapidly than average, as are larger regional firms. Between 1975 and 1980 (see Table 2.3), medium- and larger-sized companies grew faster than the national average, with the fastest growth evident in firms employing more than five hundred but less than one thousand employees. By 1988 the firms with more than one thousand employees were experiencing the most rapid growth. With the proliferation of firms of all sizes, NATS stopped publishing company data according to employment size. In late 1993 there were more than four thousand temporary help companies operating sixteen thousand temporary help offices in the United States.[20]

Occupational Segmentation

There are five major occupational sectors within the temporary help industry (see Table 2.4). In 1992, according to NATS, the clerical sector remained the dominant sector, accounting for nearly half of

Table 2.3 Size of Temporary Firms, 1975–1988 (in percentage)

Number of employees	1975	1980	1988	Absolute percent change
1–19	44.5	36.8	38.6	10.1
20–99	40.8	38.7	35.6	10.1
100–249	10.6	18.3	18.7	16.3
250–999	4.0	5.9	6.6	15.7
1,000+	0.3	0.3	0.5	17.9

Sources: Bob Whalen and Susan Dennis, "The Temporary Help Industry: An Annual Update," p. 2, reprint from *Contemporary Times* (Spring 1991); Louis Silverman and Susan Dennis, "The Temporary Help Industry: Annual Update," p. 2, reprint from *Contemporary Times* (Spring 1990).
*Percent change in the absolute number of establishments, compounded annually.

the industry's payroll. Because of the increasing prominence of executive and other highly trained workers employed on a temporary schedule, NATS recently added "professional" to the industry segments it monitors. Among the nine managers of clerical and industrial temporary offices I interviewed, six indicated that at least 70 percent of their business was in the office-related area. Only one of the nine said that clerical assignments accounted for as little as 50 percent of total temporary assignments.

Table 2.4 Industry Sectors by Payroll, 1992

Sector	Percentage of total industry payroll
Clerical	46.6
Industrial	27.5
Technical	10.2
Medical	8.8
Professional	5.3

Source: Telephone interview with Bruce Steinberg, NATS spokesperson, November 19, 1993.

Temporary Help Firms: Some Examples

Manpower, Inc.

Founded in 1948, Manpower, Inc. is the largest provider of temporary help in the world, employing more workers, operating more offices, and generating more annual revenue than any other temporary help supplier. Its national headquarters are in Milwaukee, Wisconsin, with the international base located in London. In 1975 the company became a division of Parker Pens. By 1992 Manpower's sales had reached $3.2 billion, up sharply from $300 million registered in 1975. In the period 1988–1992 the company was experiencing an annual sales growth rate approaching 7 percent.[21] Since the mid-1980s Manpower has employed more than 500,000 workers annually (200,000 more than either General Motors or International Business Machines [IBM]). In 1992 Manpower had 560,000 employees in the United States.[22] In one southwestern city where I conducted participant-observation research, Manpower managers reported that their two offices together contracted with two hundred clients annually and employed an average of three hundred workers weekly.[23] A true multinational, the company operates approximately one thousand four hundred offices spanning thirty-five countries.[24] Moreover, by the early 1980s Manpower was garnering 60 percent of its sales abroad, a world market share estimated at 15 percent.[25]

In early 1985 Manpower demonstrated its continuing intention to expand internationally when it opened its first office in mainland China. Manpower, which already had a heavy Asian presence with offices in Japan, Hong Kong, Singapore, and Malaysia, moved into China after agreeing to a joint venture with the Chinese government. The new unit, called Manpower Joint Venture Company, is based in Beijing. Like the U.S. offices, the purpose of the Chinese unit is to provide clerical and technical workers to Western and Japanese companies operating in China. CEO Mitchell Fromstein said at the time of the agreement that the entry into China "begins to move us into areas we didn't think we could ever be in."[26]

Fromstein, probably the most quoted figure in the temporary help industry, is highly regarded by business and financial observers. He was in charge of advertising at Manpower until 1976, when the company's founder sold 80 percent of the company to the Parker Pen Company for $28 million. Over a period of seven years, the original investment returned $178 million in operating income. Under Fromstein's management Parker Pen's temporary help business outgrew the writing instrument division that originally made that company famous.

In August 1987, with the financial backing of National Westminster Bank P.L.C. (Britain's biggest commercial bank), Manpower was taken over by Blue Arrow P.L.C. for $1.3 billion. The takeover made Blue Arrow the world's largest employment services company. It also led to the location of the company's headquarters in London and to a management shake-up. Mitchell Fromstein was temporarily relieved of his position atop the company in favor of Antony Berry, head of the much smaller Blue Arrow. However, after complaints from franchisees, Fromstein was reinstated.[27]

What separates Manpower from many of its competitors is its attempt to offer, and capitalize on, limited training to "qualified" temporary workers. As the chapters on clerical and industrial workers will indicate, there are few formal requirements for most temporary employees, and the majority of them work at unskilled and semiskilled jobs. However, with the adoption of various word processing systems, there is a need to reorient existing skills among clerical workers. Manpower's training program is similar to one offered by Kelly Services in that both are restrictive in scope. Indeed, both are designed to be effective after a few hours to two days of instruction.

During 1984–1985 Manpower spent $6 million developing and implementing its Skillware training program. The instruction involves the use of basic-, intermediate-, and advanced-level computer diskettes to provide simulated training experience on specific equipment. Manpower installed IBM equipment in all offices and used it to train personnel. First introduced in 1983, the program has now "trained" tens of thousands of office workers in office automation skills and has been translated into eight languages for international use. According to an IBM publication, the Skillware training program was a major factor in China's decision to select Manpower as its partner in establishing the first temporary help company there.[28] In the early years, according to Manpower estimates, the full two-day training session cost $10 per trainee.

But the program is hardly an altruistic one. According to executives with the company, the main motivation in offering training was to position the firm as the dominant supplier of word processing operators. As more companies switched from using typists to using word processors, it was a matter of either retraining clerical workers or allowing Manpower's clients to go elsewhere. As Fromstein noted, "It isn't that we're in a new business so much as that we're protecting the old one."[29] Furthermore, whereas private consultants can sometimes charge an employer as much as $600–$800 to train an individual employee on a word processor, Manpower plans to train fifty thousand to one hundred thousand temps annually at a cost of less than $30 each.

Moreover, providing some training means that Manpower can justify charging higher fees—20–25 percent more for a word processor than for a typist. National data corroborate this advantage. In a recent year the average hourly wages paid by temporary firms were $6.75 for an entry-level word processor compared with $5.50 for senior typists.[30]

But despite much publicity, both workers and industry observers have criticized the training. Temporary workers have complained about insufficient time to learn the material contained in the training program. John Kirk, editor of *Inside Word Processing* (an office automation newsletter), claimed that temporary word processors "aren't proficient at all. Manpower's people aren't going from nothing to major. . . . They're going from nothing to buck private."[31] And one user of temporary services argued that "often, the training is just a quick one-hour tutorial and handbook. My department heads require a temporary to be up and working—not spending half the time flipping through some chart."[32]

Kelly Services

Kelly Services, founded in 1946 and headquartered in Troy, Michigan, ranked, according to *Forbes*, as the largest temporary help company in the United States as the 1990s unfolded.[33] In 1991, the firm had $1.4 billion in sales, employed an average of 550,000 temps annually, and owned and operated 950 branch offices.[34] Although growing more slowly in the early 1990s, company revenue advanced between 1979 and 1989 from $369 million to $1.38 billion.[35] In early 1990 *Forbes* ranked business service and supply companies in the United States and placed Kelly atop the list.[36]

The company often takes an aggressive leadership role on matters of industrywide importance and public relations. In the mid-1980s, for example, Kelly launched a $1 million advertising campaign aimed at elevating the imagery surrounding the use of temporary help. The ultimate objective of the campaign was to demonstrate how temporary workers could be used beyond traditional occupational contexts. The ads, carried in the *Wall Street Journal, Business Week, U.S. News and World Report,* and *Working Woman,* reflected the desire of large firms to stimulate demand rather than merely relying on supply-side factors to expand their position in the U.S. economy. In another public-relations effort, the firm sponsors local "Kelly Weeks," a time when "Kelly Temporary Service renews its role as a corporate citizen."[37] During Kelly Weeks the firm dispatches workers free of charge to charitable organizations such as the American Cancer Society and the Muscular Dystrophy Association. Such techniques are effective in deflecting attention away from the firm's exploitation of its employees.

Kelly has also pioneered innovative tactics to recruit new sources of temporary workers. For example, in 1987 Kelly inaugurated a program called Encore to attract older workers. In 1989 the company employed fifty thousand workers aged fifty-five or older, an increase of fifteen thousand in just two years.[38]

Like Manpower, Kelly has tried to stake out a major part of the temporary help market by heavily advertising its "training" programs. In conjunction with Microsoft, Kelly provides training for eligible workers in software use. The company trains and supports temporary employees on a variety of word processing and spreadsheet software packages. The firm has always tried to attract and retain women workers. In this public-image–minded firm, 30 percent of corporate officer positions are held by women.

In 1991, of Kelly's 950 branch offices, 800 were operating in the

United States, together with 150 more in locations such as Canada, England, France, and Ireland.[39] In one southwestern U.S. city in the mid-1980s, Kelly's two offices maintained a clientele that surpassed one thousand one hundred employers while supplying a weekly average of three hundred temporary workers.

The Olsten Corporation

The Olsten Corporation is a North American network of more than five hundred corporately owned, franchised, and licensed temporary help offices. During the mid-1980s Olsten employed nearly two hundred thousand temporary workers annually. The company contracted its employees to more than sixty-five thousand clients and was adding new franchises at a pace of more than thirty each year. In 1991 it became the country's third largest provider of temporary workers.[40]

The company was founded in 1950 by William Olsten, who until his death in late 1991 retained the title of chairman of the board. The Olsten Corporation has been publicly traded since 1968 and has been listed on the American Stock Exchange since 1982. Following national economic and industrial trends, the company has seen significant growth in recent years. Corporate revenues for the company hit $1 billion in 1992, with net income rising to more than $21 million. In 1992 Olsten employed 321,000 workers.[41]

Generally Olsten has outperformed many of its competitors in recent years by proving more resilient in the face of cyclical swings in the overall economy. The growth of its health care division helped partially offset the effects of the recession in the early 1980s. In 1982, for example, Olsten's revenues grew 6 percent, while the nation's economy faltered. Between 1988 and 1992 sales advanced at an annual average of more than 17 percent.[42] One indicator of the intensely competitive nature of the temporary help industry is Olsten's refusal to provide information about the number of workers it employs or the number of employers it serves to a business publication surveying temporary worker use.[43]

Factors Contributing to Industry Growth

According to NATS, the industry's rapid growth is attributable to "sound, understandable macro-economic reasons." The industry's trade association explained the growth this way:

> There is a chronic shortage of skilled clerical and technical help in this country. . . . Rapidly changing technology in both the clerical and technical fields have created new skill requirements to which the workforce in this country responds slowly. . . . The result of these factors is that employers are taking longer and longer to fill their permanent job openings. In some instances, these jobs cannot be filled at all in the classical sense. . . . The temporary help industry has responded to these phenomena by helping American industry bridge the shortfall in their permanent staff.[44]

In light of the recent history of the industry, several contradictions emerge from this interpretation of the growth in temporary employment.

Although it is certainly correct that changing technology creates new skill requirements, the preceding statement creates a misleading impression about the relationship between skill requirements and new technology. Most temporary clerical employees perform semi-skilled secretarial tasks. Furthermore, as the training programs of both Kelly Services and Manpower illustrate, the new technologies generally appear to demand only six to eight hours of training and no more than two days at the outset. Finally, to suggest that the temporary help industry has simply responded to supply factors ignores the aggressive marketing role that the national and state associations have played in promoting the use of temporary workers.

Indeed, when temporary help firm managers were asked about the expansion of temporary work and the reasons behind it, they frequently cited the role of the national and state associations. For instance, one manager said the industry is growing because "business is much more aware of the opportunity and advantages of using temps. The state and national temporary service associations have been central in awakening public awareness." Another commented, "The growth of the industry has been aided by the national and state-level trade groups. These groups are active in trying to raise the consciousness of employers about the desirability of using temporary help services." Yet another manager expressed the view that "temporary work is expanding because employers have finally gotten the message through extensive public-relations campaigns by the state and national associations that there is any number of ways to make effective use of temps." In short, the temporary help industry's extraordinary growth is not driven entirely by supply-side factors; it is also attributable to the industry's demand-side efforts to aggressively market the advantages to employers of using temporary workers.

Among temporary help managers the role of temporary services in saving employers money, especially fringe benefits, was also cited as a critical factor in the growth of the temporary help industry. One manager who complained about "picky" workers collecting unemployment insurance said, "It's the economics that keep employers using 'temps.' . . . Having a worker who is eligible to receive 52 weeks of unemployment compensation is just the pits." Other managers echoed a similar rationale. One observed, "The reluctance of employers to hire permanent workers has increased much more since the recent increase in the Unemployment Insurance fund. The tax surcharge has made employers think twice about additional workers. They fear recessions and being stuck with workers and unemployment compensation premiums."

Despite the national economic expansion that characterized most of the 1980s, managers continue to believe that employers remain fearful about recessions. As one remarked at a high point in the expansion:

> Employers are still very concerned about the prospect of another downturn in the economy that may leave them with high overhead costs. Instead of having that problem, they are moving more to temporary workers. They can keep their costs, especially fringe costs, down with the use of temps. In short, the major reason for growth has to do with maintaining a lean payroll . . . to avoid overstaffing.

Against a backdrop of generally lower interest, inflation, and unemployment rates in the 1980s this reasoning remained largely intact. A temporary help firm in a rapidly growing western city placed an advertisement with the following copy in the city's largest circulation newspaper, asking (from the employer's view), "Should I hire temporary or full-time employees this year? Consider: Temporaries only work as needed. . . . Benefit costs are less. Unemployment claims are shifted. Payroll taxes are shifted."[45]

Temporary branch managers reported the provision of a low-wage, "flexible" workforce for employers as a pivotal factor in the industry's recent growth. This function will be examined in more detail in the concluding chapter.

Beyond savings in the cost of fringe benefits and the economic expansion of the 1980s, temporary employment has grown for other reasons. One manager of a large regional firm demonstrated unusual insight into the sociology of work and labor markets in identifying one possible explanation for this robust growth:

> Temporary work is also growing because of the increase in job dissatisfaction. Workers are not staying with employers as long as they used to. They are more willing than ever before to move across the street or town for small change. Automation has exacerbated this trend. Mechanization and automation have reduced the skill content of many occupations and turned more positions into boring ones. . . . The temporary help industry helps workers because they get a chance to job-hop and break up the monotony of everyday work life.

Although this interpretation contributes to the overstatement of supply-side factors in explaining industry growth, this manager accurately highlighted the boredom and declining skill content associated with many jobs. This perspective is consistent with the one articulated by many temporary workers, who suggested that temporary firms could serve as a way for them to reassert control over some aspects of their immediate working lives.

In sum, the industry stresses supply-side factors in explaining the growth of temporary work. Much of the industry literature suggests that "leisure seekers" and "insecure housewives" searching for reentry into the labor force were major catalysts in the industry's growth. To a far lesser extent, the literature identifies the role temporary firms play in reducing labor costs as a major factor.

The Future of the Temporary Help Industry

When asked to speculate about the future of their industry, managers of temporary help firms frequently converged in their responses. One common prediction was that the industry was going to become increasingly specialized over time. New and rapidly growing specialties identified by the managers included medical-related and technical temporary firms. The National Association of Temporary Services reported in 1991 that technical temporary companies now account for more than 12 percent of all temporary employment.[46] Temporary technical workers are disproportionately profitable for temporary companies because they can charge employers higher fees for more highly skilled workers.

Among suppliers of technical temporary workers in the United States are CDI Corporation and Tadtec. The largest firm among technical providers of temporary help is Philadelphia-based CDI, which had approximately 150 offices nationwide in 1990, with annual revenue approaching $900 million.[47] Tadtec, founded in 1956, is the second largest technical temporary provider, with revenue of $500 million for 1992. Tadtec has steadily increased its number of offices, often by acquiring smaller, independent companies. In late 1993 the firm employed nearly ten thousand temporary engineers and other technical workers.[48]

The fastest-growing part of the industry comprises medical-related temporary help providers. According to NATS, 11.5 percent of all temporary employees work as nurses, lab technicians, and other health-care specialists. Some medical-related workers are not medical personnel per se but rather clerical workers versed in administering medical offices and completing medical insurance forms. One of the bigger firms in the field is Medical Personnel Pool, a division of the Fort Lauderdale–based Personnel Pool of America (owned by H&R Block). Bolstered by an aging America, Medical Personnel Pool increased sales revenue 15–20 percent yearly in the late 1980s while operating more than 250 offices nationwide.[49]

Beyond these two new areas of expansion, the industry is optimistic about gains in other areas as well. The chief executive of one nationwide chain speculated that companies will "develop markets for temporary travel agents, teachers, bank tellers, beauty operators, artists, and doctors. In the next decade, companies will provide skilled people for short periods of time in basically every category."[50]

In addition, managers forecast the proliferation of new staffing strategies involving the use of temporary workers. Two such trends recently emerged. The first is known as planned staffing. This essentially involves the use of temporary workers on a kind of semipermanent basis. With planned staffing a company maintains a core of permanent workers surrounded by a buffer (sometimes called a core-ring strategy) of temporary workers who absorb seasonal or cyclical fluctuations in business activity. One manager described planned staffing as the policy of "cutting to bare bone your permanent staff and then hiring temps as business picks up. . . . The idea is to avoid overhiring and subsequent layoffs, to avoid the economic penalties that come with hiring employees on a permanent basis." Nearly all the temporary managers mentioned some variant of the planned staffing approach as a significant new trend but were rather polarized about whether it generally meant cutting permanent staff to the bone or maintaining a solid core of permanent employees.

The other new trend that managers expect to expand is the "payrolling service," or employee leasing. The payrolling concept involves an employer recruiting, screening, and training a worker or workforce and then simply turning these workers over to the temporary firm's payroll. This allows the employer to select the workers it wants at the outset while still being relieved of benefit costs and additional administrative burdens. Temporary firms typically offer discounted fees to employers under these arrangements because the agencies do not have to recruit workers themselves or incur related personnel expenses.

Managers also suggested other future trends. One innovative approach has been sparked by the often cumbersome hiring practices of large bureaucratic organizations. Several managers mentioned the practice of employing temporary workers to circumvent hiring freezes in particular and the intricacies involved with hiring full-time workers in general. Other managers spoke of their expectations for their industry's future with reference to its changing demographic composition. For example, with the aging of the population, more retirees are becoming a part of this rapidly growing sector of the labor force.

In sum, the industry and its labor force are growing much more rapidly than the rest of the economy by most measures. Whether evaluated in terms of revenue, profits, or employment growth, the industry has been one of the fastest-growing segments of the U.S. economy for two decades. The continued growth of temporary employment in a period of extended recovery seems inconsistent with the notion that employers use contingent workers during periods of contraction. Employers still reported being sufficiently anxious about continued economic recovery to resist hiring permanent workers, even after more than seven years of economic expansion. As such, they are unlikely to ever overcome their apprehension, which is possibly one stimulus behind the profound restructuring of the American workforce.

Furthermore, this chapter has begun to develop an explanation for the industry's rapid acceleration. Thus far I have explored one perspective. The temporary help industry's interpretation of its growth posits supply-side factors as central causal factors. The industry consistently ignores its own activity in encouraging, perpetuating, and expanding temporary hiring practices.

Having provided a fairly complete view of the industry with a wide angle, I now turn to the issue of how individual firms operate on a day-to-day basis. An important point is that temporary help companies do not provide a service that is mutually beneficial to workers and employers. By observing these companies' organizational structure and daily procedures, we can see that the temporary help industry exists to serve employers, while workers' needs are routinely neglected.

The Formal Organization of Temporary Help Firms

Temporary help supply companies are unique in the formal, structured way they provide temporary employment. The temporary help firm screens, tests, evaluates, and sometimes trains applicants and then offers them to business customers as uniform but flexible units of labor. The transformation of workers from full-time job seekers into mass-commodified temporary employees is facilitated by the thoroughly bureaucratized character of most temporary help companies. As noted in Chapter 2, the most rapidly growing temporary firms are large companies. These national and regional franchise firms also tend to be the most rationalized. In a calculated manner they channel applicants through an evaluation process that is designed to produce predictable, reliable, and, most important, flexible temporary employees. For most of the workers, the process is depersonalizing. The bureaucratic organization of the firms reduces the importance of individual differences.

Temporary help companies exhibit bureaucratic characteristics in several ways. For example, common organizational features, including specialization, hierarchy of authority, a clearly delineated division of labor, and a heavy reliance on written rules and records are important to most temporary companies. Among these bureaucratic elements, specialization is particularly key and warrants closer scrutiny.

Specialization

Compared with other contexts where temporary employment is found, specialization is stressed heavily by the temporary help industry. Indeed, the industry itself is highly specialized by the type of temporary help services offered. Most firms have one or two specialties, typically clerical and light industrial workers. However, many firms are far more specialized, as one canvass of twenty-four firms revealed.[51] This survey showed that companies specialize in supplying the following types of temporary workers: accounting personnel, engineering and technical workers, word processing and data-entry clerks, printed circuit board designers, drafters, medical office personnel, medical assistants and nurses, and marketing workers.

Many temporary supply companies do not attempt to provide a full range of workers. Instead, they seek to secure a niche in the marketplace by specializing in specific kinds of occupations. Most of the managers I interviewed were largely employed by companies that provided clerical and light industrial workers. However, I did interview managers of companies that supplied technical workers (drafters, engineers, and chemists) and medical-related workers (nurses aides, lab technicians, and dieticians).

In addition to the industry being segmented by type of worker offered, occupational specialization plays a further role within each temporary company. Specialization in this sense is key to the success of individual temporary firms because an employer's ability to obtain specialized help is widely advertised as an advantage in using temporary help. As Selma Friedman suggested, clients are reluctant to "pay for a temporary secretary when the job merely requires a less costly receptionist."[52] Occupational specialization has played a central role in the emergence of a mature temporary help industry because it provides one way to reduce costs. Rather than pay a relatively higher wage to a worker with advanced general skills, employers save by distributing work among several lesser-paid workers with more narrowly focused skills. Thus, specialization has played a fundamental role in the success of the temporary help industry because it provides an immediate way for employers to save labor costs.

Specialization is also important to the operation of temporary firms as each has a permanent staff responsible for the pool of specialized workers. Although many temporary offices are part of a regional or national network, individual offices are usually small, with just a handful of full-time staff members. Nonetheless, within temporary supply companies positions are hierarchically organized with specialized functions outlined for each.

Depending on the size, within the typical temporary help company there are a branch manager, one or more assistant managers, "counselors," dispatchers, and clerical support staff. The branch manager, in charge of overall administration, occupies the most prominent position within the organizational hierarchy. Generally this individual's responsibilities include preparing reports, performing accounting activities, and training permanent staff. Aside from these formal duties, the branch manager has two main concerns—soliciting and retaining clients and recruiting workers.

Worker Recruitment

Recruiting temporary workers is similar to that of other sales jobs. The manager must sell to prospective employees the idea of working on a temporary basis. As one manager expressed it, "Working as a temp can be very demanding and the rewards are slim, but to recruit you have to do a selling job." This same manager added that to recruit effectively, a manager has to overcome a "social work mentality." In other words, the worker's interests must be ignored or regarded as a secondary priority. For example, successful managers must discount workers' needs for steady employment with adequate wages and benefits. In this approach to their business, temporary help supply companies are clearly not acting in the mutual interest of workers and employers, which is a frequent refrain articulated by employers and temporary help industry representatives.

Most temporary firm managers I encountered said that "they will do whatever it takes" to recruit workers. Generally, temporary help companies prefer to hire workers who have been referred to them by other workers in the existing pool. For some firms this is the source that provides the largest number of new workers. But more important, for just about all companies it is the most effective source for obtaining *reliable* workers. Most of the firms pay worker referral bonuses to encourage this type of recruitment. To qualify for the bonus, the worker who makes the recommendation normally must wait until the newly recruited temporary employee has completed eighty hours of temporary assignments. Interestingly, information gathered from temporary workers and from managers of temporary help companies shows that referral bonuses are the "fringe benefit" received most frequently by temporary employees.

In addition to worker referrals, temporary firms use other methods to stimulate walk-in applicants. Help-wanted advertising is used both to recruit directly and to project and maintain name recognition. Some of the larger companies advertise in the mass media, whereas smaller operators rely more heavily on less expensive media such as posters, fliers, and pamphlets. Whatever the medium, all these types of advertising attempt to communicate the "advantages" of being a temporary worker. Flexible workweeks and quick paychecks are frequently highlighted.

Some temporary supply companies are more aggressive in expanding their pool of workers than others. For example, one temporary firm took the initiative of busing homeless persons from a local Salvation Army facility to enlist them for temporary jobs. According to managers involved in this case, the technique proved unsuccessful because the workers were too "unreliable" and transportation was problematic. (In the same city a majority of the homeless were already making use of alternative temporary hiring arrangements, such as labor corners and state employment offices.)[53] Nonetheless, this example illustrates the effort some firms will make to generate a large pool of temporary workers.

Other firms take a decidedly more subtle approach to recruiting, preferring methods they anticipate will benefit their companies in the long, rather than the short, run. One temporary help administrator routinely schedules lectures to high school students on job-hunting skills. In the process of offering advice on matters such as how to handle interviews and develop a resumé, the manager drops suggestions about working as a temporary employee. Another manager stresses the use of community public-relations programs. This executive's company sponsors an annual fashion show designed to heighten name recognition and offers job-hunting classes that are designed, in part, to recruit more workers.

Worker Screening

A disproportionate number of temporary help companies are owned and controlled by regional and nationwide chains. Manpower, Kelly Services, Olsten, and other temporary help chains attempt, just like other nationwide franchises (such as fast-food restaurants), to ensure that their product has uniform qualities. One way companies that supply temporary workers attempt to create this uniformity is through the screening process. At most temporary firms the screening process is pivotal in terms of recruiting and retaining the "right kind of worker." Simply put, recruiting the right kind of worker translates into *screening out* "problem" and "risky" workers. Problem workers, an employee category recognized by all the managers interviewed, are "complainers." As one manager expressed it, "We don't want complainers. . . . We don't want people who are going to speak out about wages or working conditions, just people who are confident and willing to work."

Some managers used more earthy phrases, such as "assholes" and "political fanatics," to describe problem workers. Complaining about workplace conditions to clients or to permanent workers was a major issue mangers identified when discussing problem employees. Managers want workers who will promptly show up for an assignment, perform the required tasks, and mind their own business. Managers do not want workers who object to the work being performed or the uncertain workplace environment in which it occurs.

Beyond complainers, the problem worker label also includes workers who fail to conform to the temporary firm's expectations in terms of appearance or attitude. One firm I investigated used an elaborate, multidimensional process to screen its potential workforce. Part of the regimen included assigning scores (from plus three to minus three) covering domains such as "grooming," "conversational ability," "ability to resist being frustrated," "attitude," "ambition," and "maturity." If an applicant did not score at least zero using this scheme, there was little chance she or he would ever be assigned temporary work. The manager who utilized this method did not feel that the screening instrument's objectivity was problematic despite its heavy focus on subjective criteria such as attitude and maturity.

The screening process is also aimed at preventing the firm from becoming obligated for expensive financial commitments. By eliminating risky workers, temporary firms hope to minimize their expenditures for unemployment insurance taxes and workers' compensation premiums. By examining a potential employee's work history, temporary help companies attempt to uncover any periods without work when unemployment insurance might have been collected. And by asking questions about how much weight an applicant can carry, temporary help firms try to filter out workers who may be potential health risks. The screening process also generally includes a battery of questions about past illnesses and injuries to help determine potential riskiness. Finally, as has been discussed by Heidi Gottfried, there are gendered expectations involved in worker screening.[54] Temporary help firms screen applicants for particular

assignments based at least partly on prevailing occupational stereo-
types. Screening out workers is usually the responsibility of a temporary help supply company's counselors and dispatchers.

From the workers' perspective, a detrimental effect of this meticu-
lous screening process is the creation of a large pool of applicants
who are seldom, if ever, called for a temporary assignment. The
counselor is responsible for "cooling out" these workers over time,
which means gradually discouraging them from calling for jobs by
withholding assignments. Interestingly, workers who are deemed
risky, problem, or otherwise unacceptable are generally not informed that they have fallen short of the company's standards. They
are not told what areas they would need to improve in order to be
acceptable to the company. Instead, dispatchers at many temporary
help companies simply allow hopeful workers to call in for several
days but neglect to dole out any assignments. Meanwhile the worker,
who could be job hunting elsewhere, is wasting valuable time waiting for a temporary opportunity. The permanent staff assumes these
workers will quickly lose interest and look elsewhere.

When queried about this practice, several managers indicated it
was not their responsibility to assist "inadequate" workers in any
way. Time and again managers reminded me that temporary firms
were not employment agencies but providers of business services.
As for-profit enterprises pursuing the bottom line, these agencies
reject the notion that helping workers is their responsibility. One
counselor who worked for a major temporary company told me that
occasionally she deliberately misled "unqualified" applicants by tell-
ing them to apply at another firm where "they have all the work they
can handle."

Soliciting Business Clients

Although large temporary supply companies have a network of corporate offices to support them, the temporary manager is the individual responsible for drumming up the bulk of clients for respective
firms. Recruiting clients is a very competitive process that has been
altered as the industry has changed. Compared with the industry's
earlier years, the use of annual and sometimes exclusive contracts

between temporary firms and employers is now an increasing practice. One factor that propelled the transition toward annual contracts was the relatively large number of high-technology companies that had long incorporated the use of temporary firms into their human resource policies. In Silicon Valley, where many high-technology employers are headquartered, the use of temporary workers is extensive. Along with a nationally expanding physical plant, these companies have taken their temporary staffing policies with them to other parts of the country. One manager remarked that the high-tech firms' practices have sharply reduced the average markup temporary companies can charge. High-tech employers initiate the contracting process by sending out annual proposals to prospective temporary firms. Interested companies submit bids, and commonly the company that submits the lowest bid receives the contract. Often it is an "upstart" temporary help company anxious for a slice of the market that underbids the others.

Complaints from more established firms about new temporary companies were common in my interviews with temporary managers. One blamed the downward pressure on profits on the upstart "sleaze" of the industry. According to this manager, the same temporary help firms that were charging more than a 40 percent markup were now agreeing to more modest fees of between 28 and 33 percent. Even though temporary help companies attempt to become the sole contractor of temporary labor for their clients, most employers prefer to negotiate with several firms to obtain the greatest savings for different types of workers.

With substantial revenue riding on annual agreements, it was not surprising to find that temporary firms often attempt formally and informally to influence contracting arrangements. One public-sector employer of temporary labor told me that managers of temporary firms had frequently asked him to have lunch or drinks to discuss business. He added that companies had offered him gifts but that he had never accepted any. Nonetheless, he believed it was advantageous for his organization to have several companies actively vying to provide temporary workers.

Some temporary managers acknowledged providing promotional gifts to lubricate the relationship between their firms and clients. Indeed, one manager told me she was frequently dismayed in her efforts to impress clients with gifts. She related how, when trying to peddle token gifts, such as an oversized clothespin with her company's name on it, she often noticed more extravagant gifts from the competition. In one case she saw a wall clock with her competitor's name on it.

Intensifying Employers' Use of Temporary Workers

Much of the day-to-day activity at a typical temporary help office is devoted to locating private- and public-sector employers that will hire temporary employees. After a temporary firm gains a foothold, convincing employers to expand their use of temporary workers becomes an important priority. When a temporary firm fills an assignment for a new client, the firm aggressively attempts to extend the scope of temporary worker usage within the client's organization. During one of my visits to a temporary firm, I eavesdropped on a conversation in which the branch manager was attempting to expand his company's foothold. Ostensibly the temporary manager was calling the client to check on a recently assigned temp. But before the conversation was concluded, the manager made his pitch for additional workers his company could supply. The firm was already using temporary delivery workers, but now the manager was making a concerted effort to add clerical workers. Despite attempts to secure annual and long-term contracts from employers, most clients of temporary help firms use temporary employees on a short-term, on-demand, as-needed basis.

Managers of temporary firms have developed other techniques for recruiting clients. One method involves using a survey or similar research instrument to uncover the kinds of workers a prospective employer might consider hiring. Once additional information about the targeted employer is gathered, the temporary firm can more precisely tailor their marketing campaign to meet the employer's specific needs. Although much work is done by phone (skill marketing and telemarketing), many managers spend two to three days a week out of their offices visiting clients, checking on the progress of existing workers, and attempting to intensify temporary worker usage among employers.

In addition to this approach, temporary firms locate new clients by obtaining information from temporary workers regarding other users. When an applicant applies with a temporary firm, questions usually arise about her or his past experiences with other temporary firms. That information can lead the agency to additional clients. One branch manager spoke at length about "milking" his temporary workers for all they were worth, meaning that he extracted as many worker and client contacts as possible.

Formalization, Rationalization, and Commodification

Formalization is another distinguishing feature of the type of employment provided by the temporary help industry. With this contingent arrangement, the connection between employer and worker has become completely formalized and depersonalized. Instead of one-on-one interaction with employers, temporary workers are faced with a highly efficient organizational apparatus that transforms them into flexible commodities.

Organizational rationalization is a salient characteristic of the entire temporary help industry. At the heart of the temporary help industry is cost cutting and profit maximization. From the temporary company's perspective, it makes little sense to save clients labor costs (particularly those associated with fringe benefits) if the agency must be burdened with them. In attempting to maximize efficiency, temporary firms exert considerable effort to ensure that temporary workers are cost-effective. In addition to the initial screening process designed to weed out risky and problem workers, for example, most temporary firms routinely challenge every claim for unemployment insurance filed by an ex–temporary worker. According to several temporary managers, there are lots of "picky" workers collecting unemployment insurance. This assertion is not supported by the more than two-decade-long decline in the percentage of unemployed workers nationwide who are eligible to receive unemployment benefits.

Despite the generally small size of most temporary help companies, the organization of temporary offices is extensively bureaucratic as indicated by a heavy reliance on paperwork, written

rules, and universalistic criteria. Often the rationalized and bureaucratized elements mesh effectively in meeting the organizational
objectives of temporary companies. For example, as part of the effort
to prevent their employees from collecting unemployment compensation, many firms record every exchange with a worker on the back
of her or his employment record. If an assignment is offered and
turned down, this interaction is recorded, as is the reason for reject-
ing the assignment. This use of written records helps employers
avoid unemployment insurance and other fringe benefit costs.
Again, these techniques reveal that the temporary help industry is
not one that mutually benefits workers and employers. It is distinctly
an arrangement that privileges employers (and the temporary help
industry) while shifting economic burdens to workers (by denying
them virtually any opportunity to receive fringe benefits).

The bureaucratic character of temporary help firms can also be
seen in the extensive use of paperwork in the application process.
Before becoming a temporary worker, an applicant normally must
complete, among others, math, spelling, and vocabulary tests. This
part of the application process often requires up to two hours. From
the industry's perspective, the screening and application processes
facilitate the ultimate objective of producing standardized units of
labor. Temporary help supply companies want to capitalize on being
able to provide flexible labor power predictably, efficiently, and inex-
pensively. From the worker's point of view, the bureaucratic features
of temporary help companies frequently mean a heightened sense of
degradation and a denial of the importance of individual differences.
For most employees, neither the temporary help supply companies
nor the clients that hire them are interested in the individual
capabilities of each worker. Instead, temps are treated indifferently,
more as pieces of equipment than as intelligent, competent human
beings.

The modern, bureaucratic organization of temporary work means
greater employment instability for growing numbers of workers as
employers restructure, maintaining lean payrolls in the face of
heightened economic competition and political conservatism. For
workers in the temporary help industry, even if a job is "assigned"
for two weeks, it may not last more than three days. Moreover, for
workers the industry is yet another bureaucracy that must be negoti-

ated daily, a third party that evaluates them, monitors them, and shapes their immediate working lives.

The emergence of a thoroughly rationalized temporary help industry composed of for-profit third-party employment providers has led to considerable confusion among those who apply to these firms. Upon applying, many workers are dismayed to discover that the companies are not in business to serve them. Most workers I interviewed had imagined that the temporary firms would recognize their existing skills and talents and utilize them fully. Many expressed resentment at finding they were just "warm bodies" (a common expression used by both workers and the permanent staff of temporary firm companies) and mere commodities. The calculating manner in which modern temporary companies transform workers into dispensable, interchangeable commodities has few parallels.

Temps recognize that they are valued only when employers urgently need them. The moment demand slackens, any loyalties are quickly dropped. To continue working the employee must remain vigilant, calling and returning frequently to temporary help firms and, if possible, to other employers. Abrupt interruptions of work assignments are a part of everyday work life for temporary employees. It is not uncommon for temporary workers to be assigned positions for one or two weeks only to be laid off midway through the assignment. For employers this scheduling flexibility reflects a crucial benefit of using temporary workers. Like just-in-time inventory-control techniques, using temporary employees means employers pay only for productive hours actually worked. Terminating assignments can mean great savings for employers and can function as a lucrative sales angle for temporary help companies. For workers the main implication is another short workweek. Many days of involuntary idleness are logged when employers retain workers strictly for the time actually involved in a specific work task.

An additional result of the rationalized organization of temporary help companies is that individual differences among workers are minimized. As one temporary manager informed me, "We try to make sure that all of the workers are the same." This leveling of personal differences is important because the employers that contract with temporary help companies want workers with predictable levels of training and skills. From the temporary companies' perspective, they want to supply workers who can fit quickly and effectively into many different positions; they do not want "workers who stand out" at the workplace. Employers stress the importance of maintaining uniform "products" for multiple reasons. On the one hand, talented workers may be raided by the client (reducing the temporary firm's available pool of workers). On the other hand, substandard workers may create an unfavorable reputation for the supplying company, diminishing its opportunities for cultivating future clients.

Depersonalization is facilitated by the screening process. Those who survive it do indeed tend to exhibit rather uniform personal and human capital characteristics. Moreover, this devaluation of individual differences means workers are rapidly becoming interchangeable. And from the employers' perspective, worker interchangeability is highly valued. As the organizational principle known as the Babbage Principle informs, interchangeability enables the managers of organizations to reap the fullest advantage of the division of labor. This advantage is fulfilled when employers "purchase that precise quantity" of labor "necessary for each purpose."[55]

Employers' use of temporary workers illustrates the Babbage Principle in that temporary help companies guarantee that they can provide the precise quantity of labor required for each job. Many temporary working assignments last just two to four hours, reflecting the use of temporary employees on a strictly as-needed basis. Not only do temporary companies provide workers for the precise time needed; they can also offer the highly specialized occupations employers request. To illustrate the advantages of using temporary companies, consider that employers routinely hire copy clerks, rather than secretaries, and do so for two to four hours instead of for an entire day or longer.

The ability of employers to flexibly adjust their workforces at will without any accountability for the associated social costs has contributed to the temporary help industry's rapid ascendancy in the U.S. economy. Meanwhile from the temporary workers' vantage point, the rationalized organization of temporary work produces several negative consequences. It means working for no benefits and less pay for performing the same work as other employees. It means a complete loss of control over their own labor. And it means far fewer opportunities for these workers to collectively organize on their own behalf or to resist their employers. Compared with many full-time workers, temporary employees experience a heightened loss of autonomy over their day-to-day work. When I suggested to the branch manager of one temporary help firm that autonomy on the job was an important aspect of worker satisfaction, I was cut off in midsentence with the interjection, "Temps have no say on the job; it's just not their place." This manager thought the attempt to convey temporary help from the worker's point of view was misguided. She insisted, "It's not a question of helping workers; it's a matter of serving clients."

Another implication of the modern bureaucratized character of temporary employment for workers is an exaggerated sense of uncertainty. With part-time and other types of temporary work, there is a greater degree of certainty concerning hours and working conditions. But with the temporary help industry, the loss of control, the loss of benefits, and the loss of individuality are all magnified. Under the organization of the temporary help industry, many adverse working conditions associated with contingent work reach a new zenith.

Conclusion

The emergence of a temporary help industry as an organizer of contingent employment represents a thoroughly rationalized third party supplying temporary labor as a commodity. There are other contexts in which temporary work can be found (such as on day labor corners and public employment services), but those situations are not arranged by for-profit third-party actors that benefit economically. Other forms of temporary work do not rest upon a sophisticated organizational network of offices servicing employers with uniform packages of labor. This new form of organization is sharply alienating to the majority of clerical and industrial temporary employees interviewed for this book. To highlight how temporary help companies contrast with other types of contingent working contexts, I now turn to a brief examination of other temporary labor markets in the U.S. economy.

3

THE EXPANSION OF CONTINGENT LABOR MARKETS

IN THE 1980S ELECTED politicians, powerful businesspeople, and government officials all hailed the ability of the U.S. economy to create jobs. As Alfred Malabre reported, "Over the last decade, the U.S. economy has generated jobs far more rapidly than most major economies."[1] The problem with this sanguine assessment is that it ignores important qualitative differences among jobs. In recent years the largest contributors to job growth in the United States have tended to be unskilled, low-wage jobs such as porters and food service workers. Occupations that are generally considered qualitatively superior, such as computer systems analysts, and that offer high wages and fringe benefits are growing more rapidly but are still providing comparatively few employment opportunities. A recent study by BLS researchers projected that these trends will continue through 2005.[2]

Instead of year-round, full-time living wage positions, much of the employment growth since the early 1970s has involved the creation of large numbers of part-time, temporary, and other types of impermanent positions. This chapter demonstrates that such contingent employment is not an isolated phenomenon confined to the temporary help industry. Instead, the practice of using contingent work has cut across a wide range of industries and occupations. The following pages provide some indication of how far the contingent economy has spread and thereby establish a basis from which to compare work in the modern temporary help industry. The discussion of contingent labor markets that follows is "biased" in that it focuses largely on occupations at the lower end of the working-class spectrum because it is in these occupations that contingent work has thus far made the greatest inroads. These examples of unconventional work arrangements reveal considerable variation in the objective conditions that characterize contingent work.

The Proliferation of Contingent Work

As noted, significant sectors of the U.S. economy depend upon a pool of readily available workers to fill jobs on a temporary basis. The occupations filled on a temporary basis span a wide continuum. There are, for example, relatively small numbers of engineers, architects, and professional consultants who work for intermittent periods of time, typically on a special-project basis. These professional hired hands often work under conditions they control or at least influence. Such autonomy distinguishes professionals from the larger pool of clerical and industrial working-class temporary employees, most of whom are at a particular disadvantage in the labor market. At the opposing end of the autonomy continuum from professionals are several types of temporary employees.

Business Services: Subcontracted Workers

In the pursuit of maximum flexibility, many employers have increased their use of subcontracted workers. In many cases contracted employees perform jobs that were previously held by workers directly employed by these same employers. With more firms offering such "services," the 1980s witnessed a heightened use by employers of contracted and subcontracted workers. From janitors to highly trained engineers, firms nationwide began replacing many of their permanent workers. The industry that provides the bulk of subcontracted workers is known as "business services." During the

1980s this often overlooked industry experienced far more employment growth than most others in the U.S. economy. Beneath the label "business services" is a diverse range of companies, including advertising, computer and data processing services, consumer credit reporting and collection, protective services, building services, and personnel services.

The typical subcontracting scenario involves a corporation paying a contracting firm to manage its janitorial or cafeteria needs. The expansion of this type of contingent work involves an intensified use of "job shops," which are often small businesses in which contract workers make or assemble parts for larger employers. For example, as competition among the major automobile manufacturers grew in the past two decades, Ford increasingly turned to subcontracting as a way to cut production costs. As Susan Helper viewed the situation:

> Subcontracting is a key element in the new competitive strategy of U.S. corporations. Large corporations can save money in the short run by buying components from small firms. In the United States, small firms tend to have lower labor costs because they are less likely to be unionized. And because small firms are usually in competitive markets, they are forced to accept lower profit margins than their larger counterparts.[3]

Helper's position suggests that the expansion of contingent work in the form of subcontracting has had, and will continue to generate, adverse implications for both small businesses and workers.

Belous offered an example of a major provider of subcontracted labor.[4] The GR Company (a pseudonym) is a major service management company with roughly 120,000 employees at three thousand five hundred job sites. The firm's annual revenues exceed $4 billion. The company offers, among other services, building maintenance and airport services to numerous clients. GR is a company that capitalized on the broader politically conservative deregulation and privatization movements of the 1980s. Today, for example, the subcontractor manages health care facilities in several correctional institutions and delivers school lunches to more than 650,000 children. The list of services GR offers for a fee grew as labor officials favored free-enterprise policies over the protection of workers.

It is difficult to estimate how many subcontracted workers may be employed in the U.S. labor force, but the number is clearly growing. The BLS, in a special survey of subcontracting patterns among selected manufacturing companies found a majority of companies surveyed using some type of subcontracting arrangement. The canvass, covering the period between 1979 and 1986, showed consistent increases among manufacturing companies in the use of subcontracting for a range of services, including accounting, machine maintenance, secretarial work, engineering and drafting, janitorial work, and trucking.[5]

Compared with other contingent workers, there is one noteworthy difference within the business service industry: as a whole, because of traditional occupational segregation, it employs more men (54.3 percent) than women. Predictably, however, women are greatly overrepresented among clerical and secretarial-type positions traditionally dominated by women in the permanent workforce, such as credit reporting and collection (71.1 percent).[6] Meanwhile they remain underrepresented in building service occupations that make up a disproportionate share of business service jobs.

Subcontracted workers do, however, share many characteristics with other employees of the emerging contingent workforce. They tend to be paid less than permanent workers, they have minimal access to fringe benefits, they are unlikely to stay with a particular business service firm for any significant duration, and they are almost never unionized. And like other contingent workers, subcontracted workers depress wages and working conditions for the working class as a whole. In particular, unionized workers (and, as we will see later, minority workers) are suffering significant occupational losses in the trend toward the increasing use of subcontracting. As a case in point, in Rochester, New York, local companies, including Xerox and Bausch and Lomb, have sought to divest themselves of their manufacturing operations and to rely entirely on nonunion subcontractors. Even where union members have kept their jobs, they have been pressured to accept concessions as their plants are forced to compete with the subcontractors.[7] Whereas the expanded use of subcontracting has been effective for employers as a way to forestall advancing international competition, it does so only by forcing smaller businesses and rank-and-file workers to bear heavier economic burdens.

In-House Temporary Employees

The expanding use of temporary workers has not been limited to the formal temporary help industry. Public- and private-sector employers are increasingly creating their own in-house temporary personnel divisions. One obvious implication of this approach by employers is that the number of temporary workers in the U.S. labor force is understated. These in-house temporary employees are listed among the regularly employed, many on a part-time basis, but not as part of the temporary help industry.

Examples of companies that have cultivated their own temporary help divisions are the Travelers Insurance Company, Lockheed (which employs retired engineers and scientists on an intermittent basis), the State Mutual Life Assurance Company, Motorola, Hay Associates Management Consultants, Union Fidelity Insurance Company and Abington Memorial Hospital.[8]

At Travelers retirees fulfill an estimated 60 percent of the insurance company's temporary positions. The pay offered to in-house temporary employers appears to be higher in some cases than that found in the temporary help industry; Travelers' secretaries were being paid $7.87 to $9.33 per hour in the early 1980s and clerks were making between $5.43 and $5.73 per hour. Despite receiving better wages than they would have from a temporary firm, they still offer savings to the company. A temporary retiree program at Harris Trust and Savings in Chicago, for example, reportedly saves $3.00–$5.00 an hour from its in-house program compared with the costs incurred using a temporary help company.[9]

At Abington Memorial Hospital in Abington, Pennsylvania, in-house contingent employees have been used since the mid-1970s. According to Janet Mason, the hospital draws from a pool of walk-in applicants.[10] Generally, they are full-time job seekers, and a promise of eventual full-time employment is often extended. The hospital retains approximately two hundred in-house workers in its pool and uses them to fill roughly three hundred distinct occupations. Except for professional specialists (such as management consultants), the hospital seldom has to go outside for temporary help. The "pool" employees who work on a full-time basis for the hospital receive 50 percent of the benefits of full-time employees, but a substratum of temporary employees, so-called relief workers, receives no benefits.

Union Fidelity Insurance Company in Trevose, Pennsylvania, has been using in-house temporary workers since the early 1970s. Two decades later the company had a staff of 190 workers employed on a temporary basis. A Union personnel representative said that in-house employees reduce costs not only by allowing the firm to by-pass temporary companies but also by possessing company-specific knowledge. Like Abington Hospital, Union avails full-time positions to temporary employees in its pool when openings occur. For the most part the insurance company uses its in-house employees for clerical work. But they are also used for professional positions such as accountants and actuaries. Although the pay is generally better than a worker would receive from a temporary help firm, fringe benefits remain problematic for these contingent workers; at Union a temporary employee must work six *consecutive* months to receive vacation pay.

The in-house temporary divisions of large corporations and public-sector organizations compete directly with the temporary help industry. Users of the in-house approach see cost savings in sidestepping temporary firms. The temporary help industry, viewing the development of in-house temporary divisions as an encroachment into its market and thus an economic threat, argues that employer-created pools "can cost clients more money." William Olsten, for instance, asserted, "While temporary help has proved to be a successful business tool, it does not necessarily follow that a company's 'in-house' temps department can achieve the same savings and results as a qualified temporary help firm."[11] Olsten maintained that significant factors thwart a company's successful operation of an in-house temporary service. Included in this litany are space needed to house and operate a service and the additional permanent personnel needed to operate it, including employees to keep records, interview and test potential temps, and place ads to recruit workers.[12]

Day Laborers

A numerically significant group of contingent workers in most urban environments is day laborers. The labor force of the infamous job corners affords employers the greatest possible flexibility in managing labor costs. Day laborers are on the bottom rung among wage earners in pay and receive no benefits. In many cities day labor employment is inadequate to provide workers with enough income to afford housing. Many temporarily employed day laborers are homeless street people.[13]

The lives of homeless day laborers have been studied in Austin, Texas. In the mid-1980s there were several formal locations (such as local and state employment services) where workers could obtain day labor jobs. A mid-1980s study of five hundred homeless individuals collected systematic data on the working conditions of day laborers. Grigsby summarized the homeless day laborers job search activity:

-Fifty-seven percent had used at least one of the job placement services available in the city.
-Of this 57 percent, 95 percent indicated that they had used the central office of the state employment commission.
-Over a six-month period, these workers exhibited an intermittent work pattern, using the state employment commission an average of thirty-two times.[14]

One parallel between temporary workers and day laborers is their inability to obtain an adequate amount of work. Both types of employees often work on a temporary basis involuntarily. Over the six-month period covered in the just-cited study, day laborers showed up at the state employment commission an average of thirteen times without being assigned any work. A full 50 percent of the homeless job seekers showed up at the state employment office a minimum of four times without being selected for work. Like the employees of the temporary help industry, street people are eager to work. Over the six-month period, day laborers sought work (from all sources) an average of forty-five separate times. Yet even these numbers cannot communicate the depth of the work ethic found among day laborers.

A more graphic demonstration of their need to work may be conveyed by describing their efforts to obtain jobs through the use of labor corners. In actuality, these are not specific street corners. Rather, they are unregulated urban spaces where prospective employers look for cheap labor and workers seek out any work available. At labor corners homeless men and women jump (into pickup trucks and vans) at the opportunity to work for the day. Those fortunate enough to find work through this dubious route often work no longer than a partial day. A full day is a bonus for many. In the Grigsby study 61 percent of the homeless individuals studied sought work at a labor corner. In fact, 50 percent of the street people showed up at labor corners at least twenty times over the six-month period covered. One morning when I observed job-searching activity at some of the corners, the vast majority of those pursuing work left without it. According to the Grigsby study, street people went to labor corners an average of seventeen times without finding work. And 50 percent showed up at a labor corner at least six times without being selected.

A more recent study examined unregulated job corners in Las Vegas, Nevada. Using nonparticipant observation and informal interviews with labor corner workers and employers as well as labor pool employers, Lawrence Wickliffe and Robert Parker attempted to shed additional light on the daily conditions confronted by a population of contingent workers largely ignored by city officials and the public.[15] Las Vegas, one of the most rapidly growing cities in the nation, has several day labor corners, with the intersection of "D" Street and Bonanza being the largest and busiest at the time of our research. Contributing to its size are the nearby locations of two formal providers of contingent labor—a labor pool that overflows daily by 8 A.M. and a state employment office that provides much of the same work found on the street. Our best estimates were that approximately 150 workers were visiting this one job corner daily in late 1991.

Many of the job corner workers expressed skepticism about using the local employment office. One said he could make better money getting jobs on the street. Occasionally deals struck by workers were better in some ways than those offered by the formalized alternatives. For example, job corner laborers did sometimes earn better pay, and several liked the idea that they could make money tax free. In addition, job corner workers could resist some common forms of alienation and exploitation by taking the initiative in deciding when and how diligently to look for work. This type of worker resistance is also found among the employees of the temporary help industry. One worker we met on the corner had five years of experience with job corners and labor pools. Sounding a familiar refrain, he argued that labor corners were better than the pools because workers were assigned arbitrarily to employers in the pools. On the corner, he continued, a worker knew what kind of employer he or she had before getting to the job site.

Generally, however, our observations corroborated those of other researchers writing about contingent work: manual, industrial work is almost exclusively male, with nonwhite, especially black and Hispanic, males being prominent. And like the Grigsby study, many of those among the homeless population are members of this mainly male labor force. Finally, health and safety risks for job corner workers are higher than for similar workers who find work through more conventional arrangements.

Clearly, it is in the interest of small-scale employers to have uninterrupted access to this reserve army of the un- and underemployed. As one employer told us, saving on labor costs was the main reason he used the corners to find manual laborers: "Paying them a little more is far better than paying a labor pool twice the salary to get the same type of worker." Employers who used laborers from job corners exhibited consistent hiring patterns as revealed through direct observation and casual interviews. For example, when possible, white employers tended to choose from among the disproportionately small but nonetheless substantial white workforce. Employers were also looking for workers dressed for manual labor—already equipped with gloves, a hat, and suitable shoes. The latter were emphasized because these shadow employers were seeking to avoid any formal liability for workplace injuries. Another employer drew a distinction between sober, clean, and neatly dressed day workers and those with a more unkempt appearance. He remarked that the latter type seldom lasted more than a couple of hours once on the job.

Even in boomtown cities overwhelmed by construction activity (as were both cities when direct observation methods were used), an adequate workweek is still lacking for all those who are actively seeking employment. While sharing some features with temporary help employees, day laborers are far more vulnerable to exploitation and harsh working conditions. For example, another author and researcher of the homeless informed me that day laborers are sometimes compensated for their efforts in cigarettes or alcohol. Furthermore, cases of employers callously ignoring or dropping injured workers at a medical facility are not uncommon. Day labor employers know they can just drive away, disavowing any legal liability for the health and safety of their workers.

Temporary Farm Workers

The conditions faced by temporarily employed migrant farm workers are quite similar to those of day laborers. The livelihood of farm workers hinges precariously on a number of factors, not the least of which is the health of a variety of crops needing annual harvesting. Like homeless day laborers, temporary farm workers have little control over their working conditions. Even full-time farm workers are one of the most socially disadvantaged groups in the labor force. As late at the mid-1980s, 1 million out of roughly 1.1 million farm workers were not covered by minimum-wage legislation and fully one-quarter lived in poverty. Ray Marshall added that they have few labor market skills, little formal education, and limited opportunities for employment in higher skilled, better-paying jobs.[16] According to the U.S Department of Agriculture (USDA), in 1990 there were nearly nine hundred thousand hired farm workers in this country earning $200 in median weekly pay.[17]

Few analysts have noted, however, that the majority of hired farm workers labor on a temporary basis. Moreover, their conditions are not accurately recorded by the Census Bureau. According to Leslie Whitener (a sociologist with the USDA), as many as two-thirds of the nation's 2.21 million hired farm workers may not have been counted among census farm labor categories "because they were not working on farms in March" when the census information was collected.[18] Using data from the USDA's 1981 "hired farm working force survey,"

Whitener found that only 37 percent of the hired farm laborers were actually working on farms in the last week of March when the regular census was taken. In other words, the farm laborers detailed in census reports are mostly full-time, year-round workers. Thus the numerically dominant number of farm workers who are employed on a contingent or temporary basis is sharply understated.

Whether a person labors temporarily on a farm, or works full time has important social and economic implications. According to Whitener's data, temporary farm workers averaged 39 days of farm work annually, compared with 218 days for full-time permanent workers. Whereas most of the full-time workers were white, male, married, and heads of households, temporary farm workers were more likely to be single, young, female, and members of households. The most striking difference was in annual income. In the early 1980s temporary farm laborers received just $1,071 on an annual basis, whereas the full-time workers earned $6,080 from their farm work.[19]

Migrant farm laborers have long been one of the most important but highly exploited groups of workers in the country's farm workforce. In Colorado, for example, an estimated fifteen thousand contingent farm workers make an arduous migration to harvest peaches. This part of the migrant farm workforce began cycling through Colorado in the 1920s. Abuses against migrant workers recorded in the early 1990s included minimum-wage violations, lack of toilet facilities, insufficient water breaks, and substandard food. Responsibility for substandard conditions has recently been pointed at the nearly eleven thousand farm labor contractors registered with the Department of Labor. The department investigated only three thousand five hundred farm labor violation cases in 1991, down from five thousand in 1988.[20] Most migrants are Hispanic U.S. citizens and residents of Texas, Oklahoma, or Arizona. As Jim Carrier observed, "They are at the bottom of the cheap American food chain. Yet, ironically, they sometimes don't have enough food to eat . . . and often are eligible for food stamps."[21] In 1990, thirty years after Edward R. Murrow's landmark documentary "Harvest of Shame" uncovered the grim realities of migrant life in the United States, reporters for the Public Broadcasting System series "Frontline" retraced Murrow's journey and found that in some ways conditions were worse today than in 1960. Roughly one million workers still follow the migrant trail, eking out a subsistence existence. In 1990 the average migrant family earned less than $6,000, and the average life expectancy among the migrants was just forty-eight years.[22]

In addition to temporary farm workers, many American corporate farmers encourage undocumented workers to migrate from Mexico and Central and South America to fill agricultural positions on a temporary or seasonal basis. Under these circumstances both laborer and employer have an incentive to keep the farm worker's employment hidden. Undocumented workers, faced with the threat of deportation if discovered, are far more likely to be victims of extreme levels of exploitation than are domestic farm workers.[23]

Guest Workers

As noted earlier, tens of thousands of guest workers through the H-2A visa program perform agricultural labor for U.S. employers on a temporary basis. For example, as the documentary "H-2 Worker" illustrated, about ten thousand workers from Jamaica are allowed to temporarily migrate to the U.S. each year to cut Florida sugar cane. Given a stronger Jamaican economy, many of those performing back-breaking labor for agribusinesses six months a year would otherwise be professional workers. But in Florida they are among the most exploited and dehumanized workers in the entire U.S. labor force.[24] When these temporary migrants have finished cutting cane, they are promptly returned to the Caribbean. Employers of guest workers benefit from their labor in several ways. These employers do not have to pay the employer portion of Social Security taxes, unemployment insurance premiums, or workers' compensation taxes. Furthermore, if Jamaican workers complain or cause trouble, the growers employers can have them summarily deported. Since the early 1980s, legislative proposals at the national level have surfaced calling for an expansion of the program to encompass five hundred thousand or more H-2A workers.

In recent years the Immigration and Naturalization Service has proposed changes that would provide even more benefits for employers of guest workers. These changes would liberalize the requirements under which U.S. farmers can request guest workers.

Currently, farmers must satisfactorily demonstrate to the Department of Labor that qualified workers are unavailable in the United States and that the employment of aliens would not adversely affect the wages and conditions of similarly employed U.S. workers. Under the proposed changes farmers would not have to make an extensive search for American workers if crops were in danger. Neither would they have to provide housing for workers. Instead, an employer could substitute a cash housing allowance.[25]

As noted in Chapter 1, U.S. farmers are known to prefer using guest workers even when other workers are available. For example, in the early 1980s many thousands of migrants were arriving from Cuba, Haiti, and other parts of the Caribbean. Seemingly, these new arrivals could have worked temporarily at agricultural positions normally filled by guest workers. Yet U.S. growers have consistently requested poor British West Indian workers. Again, these workers can be summarily dismissed and sent home (never to return to the United States) for the slightest infraction or sign of organized protest over wages and working conditions.

Although it would be an exaggeration to draw a direct analogy between the employees of the temporary help industry and agricultural guest workers, the latter do provide employers with similar advantages. Employers are aggressively avoiding any long-term commitment to a majority of their workers. And they are looking for a cheap labor force. Like most of the employees of the temporary help industry, guest workers are paid minimal wages and receive no benefits. Employers are also seeking a docile workforce, one that will work hard and not complain about conditions. Employers' pursuit of maximum flexibility creates social arrangements that produce similar kinds of employment conditions for guest workers and employees of the temporary help industry.

The case of guest workers demonstrates once again the substantial undercount of temporary employees in the U.S. economy. Clearly, many workers are employed on temporary schedules beyond those listed under the SIC that designates Help Supply Services. The large number of temporary workers that fall outside the official definition cautions us to adopt a critical stance toward the use of official statistics. In this case, relying on aggregate industry data compiled by the

BLS as the sole source of information on temporary workers glosses over important trends in both employment and working conditions.

Temporary Workers in the Nuclear Utility Industry

Temporary employees working for nuclear utilities are another group of workers not counted as "temporary" by official statistics. Nationally, a sizable number of workers are earning a living as "jumpers" or "glow-boys" in the nuclear power industry. These technically oriented employees are not assigned from local temporary help firms but instead come from contractors such as Atlantic Nuclear Services of Norfolk, Virginia (which used twenty-three thousand temporary workers between 1974 and 1984), or from reactor manufacturers such as Babcock and Wilcox or Westinghouse.[26]

The Nuclear Regulatory Commission (NRC) does keep track of so-called transient workers in the industry. According to the NRC, "transient" refers rather narrowly to workers hired and terminated by two or more employers in one calendar quarter. In scrutinizing industry data, Mary Melville found that the true number of temporary workers was many times greater than those conventionally hired by nuclear power stations. On the basis of her criteria, the number of intermittent workers jumps eighteenfold. Her conceptualization of temporary workers refers to "individuals hired and terminating once, twice, or more times, at one site or more, by one employer or more, during any quarter of the calendar year."[27]

In addition to being undercounted, this group of temporary workers has been growing rapidly in both absolute numbers and as a proportion of the nuclear power industry. Melville concluded her analysis by observing that

> temporary workers have been increasing over the years both in absolute terms and relative to the total number of individuals monitored by the nuclear power industry. We calculate that there were some 23,520 temporary workers out of 66,800 individuals monitored in 1976, or 35.2 percent of the total workforce, compared with 5,200 out of a total 44,795 or 11.7 percent only four years earlier. In addition, the 23,520 person temporary work force we have estimated is almost eighteen times greater than the 1,311 "transient" workers recorded by the NRC.[28]

The temporary workers in the typical nuclear energy power plant exhibit other characteristics common to the modern temporary help firm. For example, a diversity of occupations are filled temporarily, including electrical workers, divers (highly qualified, well-paid inspectors and repair personnel), health physicists and radiation monitors, and semiskilled workers. But it is the unskilled, lower-paid end of the temporary employment hierarchy that creates the greatest concern. Employed in considerable numbers, these workers (usually called jumpers) are responsible for cleanup and decontamination work. They are also charged with short-term, mechanically simple, but highly radioactive tasks such as plugging holes in reactor steam pipes.

Two researchers, Robert Kates and Bonnie Braine, studying the Nuclear Fuel Services (NFS) reprocessing and waste storage facility were the first to raise concerns about this group of workers. The nuclear facility operated from 1966 to 1971 in West Valley, New York. Kates and Braine found that some 30 percent of the plant's occupational radiation exposure accrued to workers with less than a day's stake in the industry, that they received wages far less than 1 percent of the total person-hours generated by the plant's operation, and that the NFS facility relied mainly on the presence of a captive labor force, including seasonally unemployed workers recruited from the greater Buffalo area.[29]

Robert Gillette, a reporter for the *Los Angeles Times*, corroborated the conditions faced by temporary employees at the nuclear facility. Like Kates and Braine, he observed that working conditions caused workers to reach their maximum level of radiation exposure (as prescribed by the NRC) within minutes of being on the job. And he reported that for "the Buffalo area's unemployed laborers, for the moonlighters, college students, and the young men recruited from small farming towns south of the city, the guarantee of half a day's pay for a few minutes work was an offer they couldn't refuse."[30]

During the facility's six-year history, the NFS employed about 170 full-time workers. Consistent with Melville's findings, over that time the proportion of temporary workers to full-time workers, along with average exposure dose, increased significantly. In 1968, 48 temporary workers were hired at West Valley; by 1971 the figure had risen to 991. This rapid expansion of temporary positions illustrates the prevalent industry practice of increasing the number of temporary workers to stay within prescribed radiation limits.

Dr. Marvin Resnikoff and the National Sierra Club also documented conditions at the facility and presented them before the House Subcommittee on Energy and the Environment. They reported that "the radiation exposures to workers at NFS were the highest in the world, much higher than predicted in the original Preliminary Safety Analysis Report."[31] Finally, Karl Z. Morgan, writing in *The Bulletin of the Atomic Scientists*, expressed his "serious concern at the growing practice of 'burning out' temporary employees." Morgan concluded that "the fact that many nuclear power plants are finding it necessary to solve the individual exposure problem of repair work in persistently high radiation areas of the plant by hiring temporary employees to spread out the dose . . . has increased . . . the overall cancer and genetic risks to the population.>[32]

This account of temporary workers in the nuclear industry illustrates several recurring themes surrounding contingent work arrangements. First, official statistics fail to capture the extent of workers employed on temporary schedules. The existing "official" data on temporary workers reflect only those employees working for the temporary help industry. As intimated earlier, these data do not include the two hundred thousand temporary instructors at colleges and universities, the in-house pools created by large employers, or temporary workers serving in the local, state, or federal government. The official statistics on temporary workers also neglect those hired directly by individuals to perform domestic and related duties within private households. Even when additional data are recorded for temporary workers, the figures often underestimate the true magnitude of the workforce, as was true for both the NRC's data on transient workers and the Census Bureau's figures on hired farm workers.

Second, temporary workers fill positions in diverse occupations. Some temps are well paid and work without economic coercion. But most temporary employees are unskilled or semiskilled workers victimized by a recessed economy and are members of a captive labor market. Moreover, the really dirty, dangerous work is relegated to the nearly invisible tier of unskilled employees at the bottom of the organizational hierarchy.

Third, temporary workers perform innovative functions for employers. For example, the use of temporary workers enables employers to displace responsibility for health and safety hazards while at the same time protecting core workers. With temps, the nuclear industry can reduce the risk of occupational radiation among its permanent employees.

Labor Pools

In between the labor corners and the thousands of temporary help companies is a distinctive type of temporary help supply company, the labor pool. These companies thrive on the lower end of the manual worker continuum, often entrapping workers in an endless cycle of day jobs and temporary housing that prevents them from escaping poverty.[33] In contrast to companies in the modern temporary help industry, the labor pools are in business to supply employers with workers capable of performing heavy manual labor. Like many of the industrial jobs assigned by the temporary help industry, working for a day labor pool typically involves hazardous, uncertain, arbitrary, and undesirable working conditions. It also usually means low wages, a lack of fringe benefits, and minimal government monitoring and protection.

According to research by the Southern Regional Council (SRC), temporary help companies often have a major impact on local economies. In Portland, Oregon, for example, of nineteen such agencies, fourteen reported annual revenues in 1987 from $600,000 to $10.5 million (p. 6). The annual average revenue for the firms was $3.5 million (p. 6). The SRC also highlighted the emerging role of the industry's "professional" and advocacy organizations, such as the National Association of Temporary Services, the Temporary Independent Professional Society, and the United Independent Professional Services as well as affiliated state associations. Importantly, the SRC report emphasized that the erosion of permanent work is occurring precisely at the time women and minorities are becoming increasingly prominent in the U.S. labor force.

In Atlanta, Georgia, Techwood Street is the locus for homeless and unemployed people searching for work. On this street, there are a half-dozen labor pools clustered in a three-block area. On any work-day morning up to a thousand men seek work there (p. 12). In this southern metropolis the number of labor pools doubled during the 1980s, paralleling developments in other Sunbelt cities.

In the South day labor arrangements emerged as traditional plan-tation and sharecropper systems grew less prominent. More recently, however, large employers have begun hiring temporary workers directly by placing ads in local dailies for "limited-period" workers. Furthermore, SRC authors pointed out that, although labor corners and migrant workers have long been a part of the U.S. economy, the creation of a modern temporary work industry is both a recent and mainly urban phenomenon.

Labor pools attract workers from among large numbers of the urban poor, mostly men, who congregate along city streets where the pools are located. For most a typical day begins between 5:00 and 5:30 A.M. (p. 26). The usual procedure is for workers to sign one of two lists: one for those who have cars and one for those without transportation. Those with cars are at an advantage; normally they will get work. First-time labor pool applicants typically must pro-duce a Social Security card and either a passport or birth certificate. Often workers must wait long periods after arriving for a work as-signment (p. 26).

Workers are queried about specific skills they possess despite the fact that most openings are unskilled. From the workers' perspective, the selection process appears arbitrary. Generally, better-known workers are chosen quickly, with many receiving assignments by 7:30 or 8:00. Most pools provide a fifteen-minute break in the morn-ing and again in the afternoon, with thirty minutes for lunch. At the end of the day additional periods of waiting are endured to turn in equipment and collect pay. By the time workers arrive at their night-time destination, it is between 6:00 and 7:00 P.M., twelve to fourteen hours after they initially set out to work (p. 27). If a worker receives no assignment, he or she will have likely waited in the labor hall for nearly five hours.

Some pools routinely recruit from among the homeless and visit shelter administrators to "inform" them about the location and pol-icies of the pools. In a survey of shelter directors, 85 percent reported that labor pools regularly recruited from among their homeless clients (p. 13). It is commonplace to see signs posted at pools in various cities listing schedules for pickups at local missions and the Salvation Army. Along these lines, the SRC noted that this practice reinforces a *Washington Times'* report that the "shelters and soup kitchens are (labor pools') prime source of able-bodied men and women" (p. 26). In Washington two companies, Tracy Labor and Labor Pro, compete for workers, visiting shelters as early as 4:30 each morning and returning throughout the day (p. 26).

No definitive numbers exist on this subsegment of the temporary help industry. But clearly the evidence collected in the SRC survey indicated substantial and ever-increasing numbers daily. In Washington, DC, 65 percent of the male residents at the Washington, DC, Office of Emergency Shelter and Support Services' shelters work, often through labor pools (p. 13). In Georgia the figures for temporary employment tripled between 1980 and 1985 (p. 14). In the early 1980s the *Wall Street Journal* estimated two million day labor pool workers nationwide (p. 14).

Some communities and grass-roots organizations have opposed the establishment of day labor pools. For example, in Shreveport, Louisiana, labor pools such as those described in the SRC report are forbidden to operate. An official with the state employment service told SRC researchers that the state closed a "casual labor pool" because "one-day kind of jobs like that keep a person from getting a regular full-time job. You are not going to make enough to live on, plus there are no benefits and it doesn't qualify you for Unemployment Compensation" (p. 17).

In Atlanta Dave Vincent organized Cooperatively Organized and Run Employment Service, Inc. (CORE) to operate a nonprofit labor pool. Beverly Blomgren, a social worker at Community Ministries and a CORE board member, said, "One of the things I hear about the typical labor pool is the arbitrary way these people are dealt with. They come in and sit down at 5 A.M. Many of them will still be there at 10" (p. 20). Blomgren continued, "The pools are growing by leaps and bounds. . . . Most of that is because of greed. Companies are turning to temporary labor so they don't have to pay benefits" (p. 21).

Two final examples of organizations that attempt to help workers escape the labor pool cycle are Project Liberty and Community Family Life Services in Washington, D.C. Project Liberty is in effect a nonprofit labor pool. Since the pool is not profit driven, workers earn and keep more of their income. Founded and coordinated by Paul Leach in the mid-1980s, the pool matches the needs of employers with unemployed and homeless workers. The organization transports workers on a bus to the job site and charges each employer $1.00 per employee as a surcharge to keep the pool in operation. Project Liberty was originally created to help refugees from the Cuban boatlift. Today it continues to serve a disproportionately Hispanic clientele; Project Liberty's workers are 80 percent Hispanic and 20 percent female. Community Family Life Services provides a similar arrangement as does Project Liberty, but its pool is predominantly black and female.

According to data gathered by SRC, fees charged to employers for temporary manual workers ranged from $4.00 to $14.56 an hour in 1987. The average wage was found to be roughly $7.00 per hour, with the highest local average found in Portland at nearly $10.00 per hour (p. 16). Most pools pay their workers weekly, but about twenty percent pay daily. The pools that pay by the day are usually larger than their competitors and tend to have the more egregious reputations for exploiting workers. These pools typically pay minimum or near-minimum wages (with no benefits).

At many labor pools the federal minimum wage is actually higher than what many workers receive after deductions. One Salvation Army manager, after seeing a check for $.43 cents, observed, "They never get any slack. I get the impression these labor pools know just how much to deduct." Many day laborers are skeptical about the pools' practices. Most of the pools deduct wages for hardhats, rubber boots, and any other equipment that workers are required to use. Despite the hard labor and low wages, it is not unusual for pools to sell overpriced gloves and used work clothes to their employees by making daily deductions. In the industry these deductions are known as "draws" and also apply to lunch and transportation to work sites.

Thus, day labor wages amount to a subsistence-level lifestyle. Take-home pay for an eight-hour job seldom exceeds $20.00–25.00. Relatively few assignments last as long as two or three days. Under these unpredictable circumstances, emergencies such as injuries or illnesses represent true financial disasters. The notion of "getting ahead" financially is a virtual impossibility. Despite the adversity of the employment arrangement and the severity of the working conditions, lesser-skilled workers with few alternatives continue to eke out a daily existence, arriving at the pools before daybreak and not departing until dark.

Women and Minorities in Labor Pools

Most of the workers employed by labor pools are males. Frequently this creates an unpleasant environment for women seeking manual labor. For example, baths and locker rooms are usually not available for women. One labor pool operator, however (Kay Sheats of the Industrial Labor Service in Atlanta), is expanding her labor pool to accommodate women. Her firm uses a separate hall for women and aggressively targets hotels and offices, attempting to impress upon them the virtues of temporary labor as a replacement for permanent workers in nonclerical but female-dominated positions, such as for maids and housekeepers. Most of the women Sheats supplies to employers are African American, as are most of the men.

Other observers critical of labor pools define them almost exclusively in racial terms. Billy Hands Robinson, a community activist in Atlanta and one of the organizers of CORE, flatly declared that labor pools are "primarily a black phenomenon" (p. 27). An analysis of the demographic characteristics of pool workers in many cities covered by the SRC tend to confirm that, although there are many white workers, the numerical majority of labor pool workers is African American or Hispanic. Moreover, pool workers and a manager of a Salvation Army shelter in New Orleans also pointed to race-based discrimination in job assignments. According to these sources, the hardest and dirtiest jobs are channeled to minority workers, whereas white workers often get landscaping or other, less arduous assignments. Other minority workers have complained that, despite following all of the rules for getting work assignments, they seldom get selected.

Professional Temps: Part-Time Faculty

In addition to truly working-class temps employed on a contingent basis, there are many other professional and semiprofessional workers employed on a temporary basis in the United States. In many contexts these "middle-class" employees are denied the advantages of being a professional because of their contingent working arrangement. One such case is the substitute schoolteacher. These educators are fully qualified to teach full time, but in many regions of the country there is insufficient demand for their services on a full-time, permanent basis. Similarly, there are many fully credentialed college instructors working as in-house part-time employees because those are the only positions available. Of course, some college instructors work on a part-time basis voluntarily. But for many there are simply no other academic alternatives for utilizing their professional skills and training.

An intensified use of part-time faculty in higher education emerged in the late 1960s and then expanded rapidly in the 1970s. According to the American Association of University Professors (AAUP), between 1972 and 1977 the number of part-time college professors grew at a 50 percent rate, while the full-time professorate grew just 9 percent.[34] As with other categories of workers, this growth figure is likely an understatement. Citing a report by the Center for the Study of Community Colleges, Lyman Grant indicated that the growth in the use of part-time faculty between 1971 and 1977 was closer to 140 percent.[35]

Overall, in 1970 there were 369,000 full-time professors (college teachers of instructor rank or higher) and just 104,000 part-time faculty. By 1980 the full-time faculty had expanded to 466,000, but the number of "part-timers" had more than doubled to 212,000, making "nearly one out of every three teaching jobs in higher education a part-time position."[36]

A survey by the AAUP in the early 1980s found that 38 percent of all faculty were part-time employees.[37] At some institutions the percentage of part-time instructors is significantly greater than these national averages reflect. For example, according to Grant, of the forty-seven community colleges in the state of Texas, nineteen employ twice as many part-time as full-time faculty members. At two other colleges the ratio is four to one.[38] Indeed, three community college systems in this state vividly illustrate the intensive (and extensive) use of part-time faculty. In the spring semester of 1985, there were 535 part-time instructors at Austin Community College, teaching approximately two-thirds of the two thousand college credit sections offered that term. Similarly, in the early 1980s Dallas community colleges employed nearly 2,800 part-timers, and Houston Community College employed 1,200.[39] More recent figures revealed that of the roughly 700,000 faculty teaching nationwide in liberal arts fields, 30 percent are part-time.[40]

Plainly, part-time instructors perform many of the same functions for their employers as do other types of temporary workers. Most important, these instructors allow employers substantial flexibility in managing their workforces. Reducing labor costs, especially expenses for fringe benefits, is a key motivating factor behind this increased reliance on part-time professors. For example, at Austin Community College part-time faculty are not only denied benefits but are also restricted to earning only a fraction of what full-time instructors are paid. As Irving Spitzberg, general secretary of the AAUP once commented, "Again and again colleges and universities have used part-time faculty members in an exploitative manner, paying them less than full-time teachers, giving them few or no benefits and little job security."[41]

In addition to these disadvantages, part-time college instructors are typically excluded from textbook selection decisions and committees that formulate policies directly related to faculty working conditions. In the same sense that using part-time faculty in an intensive way privileges the colleges that hire them, there is a similar set of disadvantages that part-time faculty members face that are encountered by contingent employees elsewhere. For example, many temporary workers cannot obtain an adequate amount of work from any single temporary firm, so they often seek work from several different companies. Likewise, most colleges and universities restrict their part-time workers from teaching a full load, thereby denying them the amount of work they need to subsist. At Austin Community College, for instance, part-time instructors are limited to teaching three sections per semester. Since summer employment is generally reserved for full-time faculty members, the maximum salary that part-time instructors could earn in the latter 1980s was less than $7,000 annually. Even assuming that many part-time workers are graduate students actively searching for full-time work elsewhere, such income is clearly below subsistence level. As a result, many part-time faculty members are moonlighters—a situation that is too often a disservice to the faculty, the students, and the institution as a whole. Part-time faculty members are hard pressed to devote as much qualitative or quantitative time to their students as full-time professors can. The expanding use of contingent workers in the economy seems more short-sighted with professionals than with other workers. Institutions of higher education that allow a significant part of their curricula to be taught by a part-time workforce may in the long run suffer a diminished capacity to deliver quality education.

Inadequate income and working hours are not the only features shared by temporary help industry employees and part-time faculty members. Interviews with both managers and workers in the temporary help industry revealed that many of the work assignments are devoid of intrinsic interest. Temporary workers fill stifling jobs for clients because they have a high turnover rate and because the industry frequently has such assignments available. Assigning temporary employees boring jobs relieves full-time workers, a strategy many employers perceive as an important morale-boosting technique for their full-time (or core) employees. Kathleen Lathrop pointed out a similar use of part-time workers in higher education, remarking that instructors are being used to staff "less desirable courses (remedial and writing courses, for example) or those offered at inconvenient times, so that regular faculty members need not be burdened."[42] Instead of altering work to make it more interesting for all workers, employers of temporary workers and part-time college professors use contingent employees to divert disaffection from among the permanently employed.

Additional similarities can be seen in a closer examination of workplace conditions. As Barbara Johnson detailed, working as a temp means getting the oldest desk, the oddest lunch hours, and the last choice in just about everything else.[43] Among part-time faculty members, analogous indicators of their low status in the organizational hierarchy can be seen in inadequate office space and supporting facilities.

Institutions of higher education that choose to increase the use of part-time faculty may be financially advantaged in the short run, but the creation of deleterious effects for workers and their students appears likely over the longer term. As Grant reasoned:

> Mediocre teaching is propagated by the overuse of part-time faculty. . . . Some part-time instructors are not primarily interested in teaching; it is something they do after a full day's work. . . . Their teaching is not as good as someone's whose only job is to teach. Furthermore, excellent teaching is not rewarded by better pay, job security, voting privileges on the task force, and certainly not by an eventual full-time job.[44]

Temporary Bureaucrats: Government Workers

Traditionally, employment with the federal government through the career civil service has meant having a "good" job with plenty of perks. Most government workers have come to expect an elevated lifestyle with higher-than-average pay, comprehensive health insurance, group life insurance, paid days off, and, perhaps most important, lifetime job security.

However, public-sector agencies, like their for-profit counterparts, are increasingly relying on temporary workers to provide their organizations with flexibility in dealing with workload fluctuations. Indeed, OPM officially encouraged the use of contingent workers in the 1980s as a way to cut costs. Consider this excerpt from a mid-1980s OPM newsletter: "Temporary limited employment is one extremely important element in a comprehensive staffing policy, and one which is very cost efficient. Recent trends in agency staffing, however, show a disturbing growth in full time permanent (FTP) employment at the expense of temporary, part time and intermittent staffing."[45]

As indicated earlier, the adoption of policies that discourage hiring full-time, permanent workers in the public sector was given a significant boost in 1985 when Donald Devine, the head of the OPM, gave all federal agencies far-reaching authority to hire and retain temporary employees without requiring them to use the competitive selection process required for permanent civil service appointments. Even before the liberalizing directive, there were nearly 245,000 appointments in a 2.2 million federal employee workforce.[46]

Today the federal government uses several types of temporary (and other contingent) employees, a practice that empowers managers with greater flexibility in addressing their employment needs. For example, the use of "term temporary employment," in which workers can be hired for one to four years, was expanded in 1987 to provide "sufficient flexibility for agencies to maintain a transitional yet competent work force."[47] Additionally, guidelines for using "temporary appointment pending establishment of a register" were changed. The enacted changes allowed agencies to hire worker-trainee positions without an examination. Although eligible for career employment, most workers' tenure is less than the three years required.

In 1989, to provide federal managers with even more personnel discretion, the OPM approved hiring employees of the temporary help industry. Already a rapidly growing industry, this major employer may provide temporary companies a major boost in coming years. Presently "temporary limited employment" is the most common form of temporary employment in the federal government. With this variant, federal agencies can fill temporary appointments with a "not to exceed" date when they get permission from the OPM "to meet an administrative need for temporary employment, such as to fill a temporary position or a continuing position for a temporary period."[48]

Many of these positions are contingent in more than one sense. The appointments cannot exceed one year, but they can also be terminated at will. Benefits for these workers are nonexistent for the first ninety days of employment and subsequently are less than what permanent workers receive. Furthermore, these workers tend to earn less because they are usually assigned the first step of a civil service grade without an opportunity for upward mobility.

Other contingent arrangements in the public sector include part-time and intermittent employment as well as seasonal and on-call workers. The government avoids hiring relatively expensive permanent part-time workers because they receive prorated fringe benefits as well as annual leave and sick leave. At the other end of the cost spectrum are "intermittent" workers. These workers are appointed one week at a time and are employed for thirty-nine hours so that expenses are not incurred for fringe benefits. The bottom line is to ensure that only time actually worked is compensated.

Conclusion

There are, of course, many other examples of employees who work on a part-time, seasonal, temporary, or some other contingent basis. Indeed, as Mayall and Nelson suggested, temporary work today cuts across a wide variety of industries and takes many forms, including the employees of the temporary help industry, "floaters," "formal intermittents," "casuals," workers from "internal pools," "contract labor services," and "independent contractors."[49] The examples presented here, although stressing less prominent and prestigious occupations, are suggestive of broader labor force trends in the U.S. economy in the early 1990s.

Significantly, the intensified use of contingent workers documented here implies an increasing number seeking permanent work as private-sector employers continue to restructure, downsize, and reorganize their companies. Yet traditional sources for such opportunities are vanishing as major employers strive to meet intense international competition. Corporations are also creating fewer full-time positions as they attempt to deal with an economic environment that was altered in the 1980s by deregulation and privatization. The negative fallout from these transformations have been particularly grave for urban minority youth. And the same forces behind the increased use of contingent workers have eroded hard-won racial victories. For example, minorities and women tend to be the "last hired and the first fired." Increasingly, the kinds of full-time entry-level occupations minorities are able to obtain are becoming a part of the contingent economy.

The following two chapters present an insiders' account of temporary work, largely by relying on my accounts of being employed as a temporary employee and through open-ended interviews with other workers and managers. The task of viewing temporary clerical work from the worker's perspective is the subject of the next chapter followed by a first-hand look at the worklife of "light" industrial temps.

4

TEMPORARY CLERICAL WORKERS

TEMPORARY CLERICAL WORKERS are central to the economic success of the temporary help industry. These workers are hired by employers more frequently than any other occupational category. In 1990 a little more than 63 percent of all temporary help assignments were for clerical-related positions.[1] According to NATS, more than 90 percent of companies with automated office equipment use temporary clerical workers at some point. Although other categories of temporary help (such as home health care workers) have been growing faster, clerical positions continue to provide the majority of the employment opportunities for temporary workers.

Why do workers take clerical jobs for employers on a temporary basis? How do employees feel about being a temporary secretary, data-entry operator, clerk, or receptionist? What are workplace conditions like for temporary clerical workers? These are some of the basic questions guiding this chapter. In large measure the answer to these inquiries stem from my experience working as a temporary clerical employee, from in-depth interviews with temporary clerical workers, and from interviews with the managers of temporary help firms.

Choice versus Economic Coercion

One prominent aspect of working as a temporary clerical employee is its largely involuntary character. Few workers prefer to be employed on any kind of contingent basis; most workers want year-round, full-time jobs. Workers choose temporary work to survive. Most employees of temporary companies share much in common with involuntary part-time workers (those who express a preference for full-time work but who accept part-time work for "economic reasons"). Among the clerical workers I interviewed, the preference for permanent employment was unambiguous. Furthermore, managers of temporary firms corroborated the fact that their employees were mainly frustrated workers searching for full-time jobs. In fact, only one of eleven managers said that the percentage of full-time job seekers might be as small as 50 percent. According to this manager, the other 50 percent are "housewives looking to supplement the family income." Representative of the belief found in most temporary firms was the comment offered by one manager that "almost all of the clerical workers are looking for full-time jobs."

Despite workers' clear preference for full-time employment, the temporary help industry has propagated a different image about the typical temporary worker. Through industry efforts a number of self-serving myths have been created and perpetuated surrounding employees of the temporary help industry. Often they are characterized as housewives with a weak labor force attachment or workers who value leisure time more than permanent employment. The following is how the leading private spokesperson for the temporary industry, Manpower's CEO Mitchell Fromstein, expressed this view:

> As housewives become aware of the labor market value of their former office skills, they cautiously seek possible work opportunities and skill measurements as the preliminary step to worklife re-entry. These women are unsure of their marketability and their real desire to work. They are inhibited in their willingness to seek or accept normal office positions but are curious at the possibility. They could best be described as job market "probers" rather than job seekers. . . . In many cases, their skills need improvement and assurance that they still have the ability to be productive and will be accepted into the workforce. They fear the classic job

interview. . . . The temporary help firm offers a suitable "half-way house" to these job seekers.[2]

In these comments, Fromstein overemphasized the role of free choice in working on a temporary basis while neglecting economic coercion as a factor causing many to rely on contingent work. Additionally, he implied that the typical woman worker is weak of character and deficient, requiring extra assistance to enter or reenter the world of work.

In a similar vein the industry publication *Modern Office Procedures* identified every type of person in its litany of temporary employees except full-time job seekers. According to this publication's account, temporary workers are "students home on vacation, retirees who would like to work occasionally to relieve boredom and supplement their income, housewives who are through raising their children and are just beginning to get back into the swing of things, and even artists and freelancers of various sorts."[3] Sam Sacco, speaking for NATS, added to the leisure-seeker mythology, claiming that "many temporary service operators . . . have noticed the emergence of a new type of employee—a career temporary—who enjoys the diversity of working in different office environments, likes picking his or her own hours, and can live on the salaries."[4] Finally, Barbara Johnson gave much weight to the role of voluntariness in working as a temporary employee. In her view, temps are employees who have "elected to be without company ties so that they can work when they want to, can consider other jobs any time they want to, and can be free to enter or leave the temporary work force."[5]

The idea that most clerical temporary workers are either leisure seekers or workers with a primary attachment to family life was not borne out by either the workers or the managers I interviewed. Most of the managers said the leisure or reluctant housewife types were 10 percent or less of their entire pool of temporary workers. All the managers were aware of the industry-propagated image of temporary workers as laid-back leisure seekers, but the majority dismissed it, describing that kind of employee as a nonexistent or vanishing breed.

Observations, interviews, and other corroborating evidence did suggest, however, that a strong, positive association exists between a voluntary choice of temporary work and skill level. The greater the skill level, the more likely the worker will be able to work regularly for a temporary help firm. Thus higher-skilled workers exercise greater discretion and autonomy about their temporary work lives. But lesser-skilled temporary workers cannot afford to be choosy and are forced by economic necessity to accept any and all assignments offered. Martin Gannon, using a mail survey completed by 1,101 temporary employees of health care companies, confirmed this relationship between skill level and the free choice of temporary employment. He found that two groups of higher-skilled workers (registered nurses and licensed practical nurses) were less likely to desire a five-day (or more) workweek than were two lesser-skilled groups (nurses' aides and homemakers). Similarly, the higher-skilled groups were much more likely than the lesser-skilled workers to cite "freedom to schedule work flexibly" as the most important reason for becoming a temporary help employee.[6] Thus, there is some truth to the notion that temps choose such arrangements freely, but those workers are in the minority. Why do most temporary employees want full-time, rather than intermittent, working schedules? Not surprisingly, most temporary employees offer the same reasons cited by permanent full-time workers. The major reasons include the desire for economic security, job stability, better pay, and fringe benefits. In fact, several workers said a part-time job is better than working as a temporary employee because of greater job security.

Moving from Permanent to Temporary Work

Most of the temporary employees interviewed for this book who wanted full-time work had had previous full-time working experience. As such, they were in an insightful position to evaluate differences between permanent, full-time jobs and contingent work. Before joining the ranks of the temporary workforce, most of the clerical workers had been full-time clerical workers or educators. Fairly typical of the workers who agreed to in-depth interviews was a woman with two and one-half years of teaching experience and one and one-half years of full-time secretarial experience. One worker had been a full-time elementary schoolteacher for the previous six years. In each of the years before the interview, she had been able to find a full-time job for the summer to supplement her income. Now unable to find other, more stable employment, she was relying on temporary firms to make ends meet.

The majority of temporary clerical workers in this study arrived at temporary help as a result of one of three sets of circumstances. Some were recent arrivals to the community and had been unable to find permanent work. Others were entering the labor market on a full-time basis for the first time and could not find full-time work. And still others were accustomed to full-time positions but were in between jobs because of resignations, layoffs, or terminations. So in my sample clerical employees worked for temporary firms largely on an involuntary basis. This was a "choice" they had made after exhausting other, more preferable working options.

Of course, some temporary employees do work on an intermittent basis without feeling economically coerced. Among the clerical workers, the ability to continue an education while earning income was the most common reason cited for preferring a temporary working arrangement. Nevertheless, among the employees who did not prefer full-time work, none cited reasons that were consistent with the industry's public-relations image. For example, none of the workers mentioned having a primary orientation to home life or wanting more leisure time.

Logistically the clerical employees who arrive at a temporary help firm after exhausting more desirable alternatives do so in a number of ways. Some prospective clerical temps got the idea to work on a temporary basis after reading help-wanted ads in a local newspaper. Another handful applied to a temporary firm after having the idea suggested to them by an acquaintance, friend, or spouse. Others applied after seeing openings for temporary work listed alongside full-time advertisements, such as those posted with state employment offices. Some found temporary offices listed in the yellow pages under "employment services." And still others began to work as temporary employees after visiting a temporary firm while searching for permanent full-time work. One clerical worker explained that she had first applied for temporary assignments as "an accident." She thought the firm was a full-service full-time employment agency. When she learned of her mistake, she decided to give the agency a try because it was "free" and "some work was better than none."

The Application Process

Workers who determine that temporary employment is an acceptable working arrangement set up an appointment and formally apply to a temporary firm. The application and screening process is of great significance from the temporary company's perspective in terms of obtaining the "right" kind of worker. From the worker's vantage point, the application and screening process is usually tedious, especially for workers who apply with several firms.

As a participant observer, I applied for temporary clerical work to three different firms. With each company the application and screening process took approximately two hours. Outwardly the process appears to be mainly concerned with skills and other formal, objective job requirements. But from the firm's perspective, the process includes a hidden agenda. Consider the comments of one manager: "Personal attributes are pivotal in filling a temporary assignment. . . . You need to consider skill level as 5 percent of your order, with the remaining 95 percent going to personality or other personal characteristics."

The application process typically includes a battery of detailed tests covering various kinds of office skills. Included are separate sections evaluating the applicant's filing ability, vocabulary skills, math, spelling, and competence on the office equipment that the applicant claims to operate. If a worker is applying to operate a calculator, a typewriter, and a computer, the process can last considerably more than two hours. The workers who applied with more than one company frequently remarked about the prolonged length of testing and the fact that it was very repetitive.

From my experience I could easily empathize with these workers' protests. For example, I took three different typing tests, and each time achieved approximately the same score. These unnecessary and repetitive tests represent "opportunity costs" to workers. For them, the application process is inefficient because most are looking for full-time work and could use the time to greater advantage.

A crucial aspect of the application process for the temporary help firm is the hidden evaluation that commences the moment an applicant steps in the temporary supply company's door. From the outset the company's personnel are evaluating the applicant on dimensions that are less than completely objective and that often have little to do with a worker's ability to perform competently on the job. The following comments suggest the flavor of this hidden evaluation:

> "If they have body odor, they're gone."
> "Can they speak well?"
> "Do they slouch in their chair?"
> "Are they dressed and groomed well?"
> "Do they seem easily frustrated?"
> "Do they seem friendly and outgoing?"
> "Are they mature?"

Without exception, managers and other permanent staff at temporary firms emphasize this "personal" side of the evaluation process. Yet applicants are largely unaware that this part of the evaluation process is under way. Instead, their attention is focused on performing well on the administered standardized tests.

Chapter 2 noted that temporary firms use the application process to screen out problem and risky workers. But what about the other side of the evaluation? What sorts of workers do temporary employment companies hope to recruit and retain through this personal evaluation process? Again, the answer surrounds the corporate search for flexible workforces. Temporary companies attempt to retain workers who exhibit maximum flexibility. One temporary manager told me, "With jobs and bosses changing all the time, you have to be flexible." Another added, "You never know what kind of situation you're going to walk into. . . . you have no idea of what to expect." Barbara Johnson agreed that this kind of personal flexibility is a key quality for the successful temporary employee. She advised prospective temporary employees that flexibility means they

> should be flexible enough in their attitudes to work as fill-ins at irregular hours and on the days when regular employees are on holiday. . . .

TemTemporaries should be agreeable to working at out-of-the-way locations and places of distant commute. Temporaries must take the odd desk, the odd lunch hour, and be flexible enough to make this seem agreeable.[7]

Later she added:

You may be assigned the least desirable desk or work space, the obsolete or worn equipment, and last choice for lunch hours. Learn to expect this. Being last in line is part of a temporary life. . . . As a temporary, you'll be moving on to a different situation soon and maybe your next job will offer better breaks.[8]

Beyond flexibility, managers said they want

-"someone who is trustworthy and dependable. . . . Malcontents are unacceptable."
-"a special kind of person . . . someone who is open-minded and willing to get along."
-"workers who are outgoing, personable, smile easily, and work well with people."

Other managers added that temporary workers "should not be too opinionated; they should keep any dissatisfactions to themselves."

Despite earnest efforts, all the temporary managers admitted allowing some unacceptable workers to slip through the screening process. One manager commented that when he finds "disruptive assholes," he tells them straight out that if they want to work, they cannot talk about bad pay and conditions. In particular, he instructs them not to talk about these issues to the full-time employees they will associate with while working on an assignment. The manager explained that sometimes "in a case like that, I recommend isolating the employee at the client's workplace."

Working Conditions

Employment Uncertainty

From the workers' perspective, there is an important flip side to the "human resource flexibility" being aggressively implemented by corporate America and championed by the temporary help industry. Workers tend to experience flexible work arrangements differently; what employers see as flexibility, temporary workers often perceive as uncertainty. Indeed, uncertainty is a key distinguishing feature of all types of contingent employment. And for many it is the most salient and pervasive characteristic of temporary work. The timing and length of temporary work assignments are perhaps the most obvious aspects of this ubiquitous uncertainty. Even among workers who reported receiving an adequate amount of work, considerable suspense remained concerning when work would be assigned and, conversely, when an extended period of idleness might ensue. One employee succinctly expressed the issue in terms of "never knowing when you're going to work and then not knowing how much work there will be."

Uncertainty surrounding the workday, then, frequently begins at the outset of each new day—with no knowledge if any assignments are available. If workers want to stay employed with a temporary firm, they must remain on-call without interruption. In this way the uncertainty of temporary work intrudes into a person's leisure time as well, blurring the boundaries between personal time and working time.

Among the clerical workers I interviewed, most said they worked an adequate amount of hours during most weeks. There was, however, a distinct minority that said they were not satisfied with the amount of work assigned. On average these workers were receiving between 5 percent and 20 percent of the amount of work they preferred. Again, manager comments corroborated the workers' assertions about the lack of certainty in obtaining adequate amounts of work. The consensus view among managers was that most temporary clerical employees had to remain active and available before they could reasonably expect to obtain an adequate amount of work.

A worker's skill level plays an important role in the receipt of adequate workweeks. As several managers indicated, there is a strong positive association between skill level and the ability of workers to garner as many assignments as desired. For example, among clerical workers general office clerks have a harder time finding regular employment than do more highly qualified full-service secretaries. Also, the ability to operate automated word processing systems helps ensure that clerical temps will receive adequate hours. In contrast, a clerk whose skills are largely limited to filing and typing is likely to have many shortened workweeks.

Among the clerical workers who reported receiving an adequate amount of work, most usually worked nearly forty hours. The rest were working an average of between twenty and thirty-five hours weekly. Despite the adequacy of hours reported by the majority of clerical temporary employees, many noted that great uncertainty persisted about the availability of working opportunities. For example, one clerical employee who had completed several forty-hour workweeks over a six-month period, and who reported being generally satisfied with the amount of hours worked, remarked that "you never really know when or how much you're going to work. One week when I really needed to have a full paycheck, I had only one assignment—four hours on Wednesday."

Moreover, even when a temporary employee is provided a working opportunity, uncertainty continues concerning the duration of the assignment. An example of this type of uncertainty arose while I was working at one of my first clerical assignments. Near the end of my first day performing clerical work with a public housing authority, there was much discussion and confusion among the other three temporary employees in my work group about whether we would be asked back for the following day. Although we were scheduled to check out at 5:00 P.M., at 4:20 our supervisor was uncertain whether there was an ongoing need for our labor. Shortly later the supervisor returned and asked us to stay "until 8:30 or so." Having arrived shortly after 7:30 A.M., I declined but offered to return the following day. The supervisor indicated that was agreeable but said she needed only two, not three, of us to stay or return. At that point one clerical temp opted not to return. A similar vignette unfolded at the end of the second day, and during a slow period on the third day, I offered to leave.

Uncertainty about the duration of assignments was a frequently mentioned source of dissatisfaction among the workers I interviewed. In most of my experiences as a temp, the employer asked me to return for additional days. But the obverse also occurs routinely. Several workers complained about being sent out on work assignments that were supposed to last two weeks only to have them cut short by several days or more. Temporary firms tell workers how long the assignment is expected to last, but most employees soon learn such information is an educated estimate at best.

Other Forms of Uncertainty

The ambiguity enveloping temporary employment does not end with the length of the assignment. Once a worker is on a job, uncertainty spreads into other domains of work, including everything from idiosyncratic work procedures, to the scheduling of breaks and lunch, to the location of workrooms, restrooms, and lunchrooms. Among the permanently employed, it is difficult to imagine a work life in which this degree of reorientation is continually demanded.

For example, full-time workers can, and do, take for granted their employer's location and the best routes by which to arrive and depart. Many temporary clerical workers do not have even that luxury. In the assignments I completed, and in many that other workers discussed, simply finding the assigned workplace was often problematic. In fact, one temporary clerical worker cited "bad, wrong directions" from temporary help personnel and "getting lost running all over town" as some of what she disliked most about working as a temporary employee. This problem is amplified among temps who have recently arrived in an area.

An assignment culled from my ethnographic experience will serve to illustrate this aspect of uncertainty. One morning I received a call at approximately 8:30 from a temporary firm that needed to fill a clerical assignment at a central-city location with a familiar-sounding address. I was told parking was unavailable in the immediate area and was instructed to park at the city's municipal auditorium and commute to the job site via bus. Despite the short notice, I was exhorted to get there as promptly as possible.

Following the bus commute, which easily added twenty minutes to my trip, I reached the block where the employer was located. Searching but never finding an address, I finally noticed a sign for a bank building that sounded like the correct destination. I headed inside, took two different elevators, and wandered around for about ten minutes before I realized, with the help of a receptionist on the sixteenth floor, that my employer was in the bank building across the street. Someone intimately familiar with the area would likely recognize the correct address and the difference between two similar sounding but distinct banking entities, but to a less experienced temporary worker, navigating to the correct location can be confounding. Once in the correct building, I was directed to the twelfth floor, to the twentieth floor, and then back to the twelfth before I located the area where I was assigned to work.

This brief vignette from a day in the life of a temporary clerical worker reveals that even minor areas of work are punctuated with frustrating ambiguity. For workers who receive temporary assignments on a fairly regular basis, this can mean tracking down two or three new workplaces weekly. It is yet another drawback to temporary work and represents the kind of uncertainty with which permanent employees must rarely contend. Full-time workers know where they are headed in the morning. They know how much time to allow for private or public transportation, whether parking is available, and where they can get lunch. In contrast, temporary clerical workers often begin their working day uninformed and confused about such routine matters.

Beyond these areas of temporary work life shrouded in ambiguity are additional gray areas. For example, each day brings new uncertainties about the character of the work itself. Will it be boring or challenging? Will there be close or loose supervision? Will co-workers and supervisors be friendly and helpful or cold and aloof? All these basic workplace conditions are unknown variables for the workers employed by the temporary help industry.

Length of Assignment

Among the clerical workers interviewed for this book, the typical assignment lasted between three days and two weeks. The longest among any of the twenty was six months. The shortest assignment was a partial working day; several clerical workers reported working assignments that lasted as briefly as a few hours. Only a handful had an assignment that lasted as long as three months. Managers agreed with this portrayal of the duration of assignments. Most cited a period of one to two weeks as the average length for a clerical assignment. Some managers noted that assignments were hard to classify in terms of average length since some lasted as long as three years, whereas others were as brief as two hours. Some suggested there was a trend toward longer-term assignments, and certainly that is a major goal of the industry.

In a study of 882 employers that used temporary help companies, Nelson and Mayall found the average assignment length to be 11.8 days.[9] The researchers found statistically significant differences in assignment length across industry sectors. For example, in transportation 45 percent of all assignments were for one to two days, and none was as long as 30 days. In the financial sector only 7 percent of the assignments were in the one to two day category, whereas 51 percent lasted between 6 and 29 days. Finally, Nelson and Mayall found that the higher the cost of benefits for permanent employees, the longer the duration of the assignment, a finding consistent with the explanation for the industry's rapid growth cited earlier. Kate Tomlin, executive director of the Texas Association of Temporary Services, and Ron Kapche, an executive with Manpower, pointed out that roughly 75 percent of all clerical assignments are for one month or less.[10]

Wages

Wages can vary considerably for employees in the temporary help industry. In my experience working clerical assignments, the pay ranged from $4.00 and $10.00 per hour. In a majority of the assignments, I earned $4.50 or less. Wages in the range of $4.00–$5.00 per hour were common among the temporary workers with whom I spoke. In fact, of those who agreed to in-depth interviews, the majority reported that the most frequent pay range was $4.00–$5.00 per hour. Only a handful reported earning, on average, $5.00 or more per hour. The relatively low pay for clerical assignments was a frequent complaint voiced by temporary workers. One young employee who was still living with her parents asked rhetorically, "What would I have done if I had to live on this?" One of the better-paid clerical workers declared, "People work to make money, but there's no way you can make money doing this; it's a rook." Several other clerical employees questioned whether temporary assignments were "worth it" after taxes and commuting expenses were calculated.

Managers of temporary firms reported a similar pay range, although they tended to emphasize the upper end of the pay scale that highly qualified secretarial employees sometimes earn. The pay for clerical workers did not vary much among different temporary firms. The highest-paying company among the nine I surveyed claimed to maintain a minimum wage of $4.75 for clerical workers. Apologists for the temporary help industry frequently assert that temporary workers earn as much, if not more, than full-time employees. For example, Teresia Ostrach, director of temporary operations with Dunhill Temporary Systems, said, "In many cases, working temporary pays as well, if not better, than full-time employment."[11] Both the primary and secondary sources of evidence presented in this book strongly suggest such assertions regarding pay are part of an industry-created and -perpetuated mythology.

The myth of well-paid temporary clerical employees has emerged for a number of reasons. First, it is true that some temporary employees are highly compensated, but most of these are technical or administrative workers. Second, some temporary companies have adopted the bait-and-switch marketing techniques (or other forms of deceptive advertising) long associated with the retail industry. Some unscrupulous temporary help operators advertise for highly paid clerical temps, but when workers apply, they are told that all the high-paying jobs are currently filled. Then the firm switches the applicants to less remunerative assignments.[12] Third, the image of the well-paid temporary clerical worker is reinforced by firms whose managers boast of "paying temporary employees a wage comparable to a permanent employee in the same position." Even when true, the permanent employee receives fringe benefits generally unavailable to temporary workers.

Of the managers who agreed to in-depth interviews, none could recall an instance in which a temporary clerical worker was paid more than a full-time employee in the same position. Most stressed that temporary employees were paid on a comparable basis with full-time entry-level workers. Usually that meant temporary workers earned at least $.50 less per hour than their permanent clerical counterparts.

Benefits

There is one area of temporary work life that is not riddled with uncertainty: fringe benefits. Temporary workers do not receive any of the perks typically earned by full-time workers, including health insurance, paid days off, and pensions. The barrier is not simply the unavailability of benefits. Many temporary firms advertise that they offer fringe benefits. Rather, few workers stay at this work long enough or consistently enough to satisfy the criteria temporary firms set to qualify for benefits. Only one clerical worker interviewed for this book indicated receiving any kind of fringe benefit. This solitary worker was employed by the temporary employment division of a major research university and after six months of continual experience earned benefits comparable to those received by permanent employees.

The policies of most temporary help firms dictate that workers complete the equivalent or near-equivalent of a full-time working schedule over an extended period to qualify for benefits. This makes it very difficult to ever earn benefits because even among clerical employees who said they were receiving an adequate amount of work, many were not working forty hours a week. To receive pay for a major holiday, one firm requires that an employee work both the day before and after the holiday, and six hundred hours within the previous six months. Another company offers vacation pay to employees who have worked fifteen hundred hours within the calendar year; in a hypothetical second year, they are eligible for eighty hours of vacation pay after completing one thousand eight hundred hours. Generally, these requirements are simply unrealistic and unattainable for temporary clerical workers.

Despite the barriers temporary workers confront in attempting to earn benefits, industry advertising continues to tout the availability of fringe benefits. For example, Mike Kutka, vice-president and regional manager of a Houston-based temporary chain, recited this litany of potential benefits as his interpretation for why the number of temporary workers has grown rapidly:

> Another aspect that has attracted new employees and increased retention has been the advent of a full line fringe benefit package, which may include paid lunch bonuses and paid vacations. . . . One temporary help service firm, for example, includes in its program: group medical, life insurance and accidental death (20% paid by the temporary help service), six paid holidays, seniority bonuses, cash and recognition awards for the "Employee of the Month" in each of its offices, and a Federal Employees Credit Union for its temporary employees.[13]

A recruiting tool used by some firms has been the establishment of so-called clubs for temporary employees. Ostensibly the purpose of the clubs is to acknowledge and reward workers who achieve distinguished longevity records. In a letter to the temporary help industry's trade association, this is how one worker described an experience with the "club" concept: "As for the extras, one of the companies I just signed with has a 'club.' Work 300 hours in twelve months and I receive a pin and certificate redeemed for merchandise. 300 hours—I haven't heard from the company yet."[14] Another firm publicizes a dubious plan in which its employees can "travel and work." At a worker's request this temporary company transfers the employment records to a branch office located near the traveler's planned destination.

The managers of firms I interviewed confirmed that temporary workers seldom receive benefits. Indeed, when I asked one manager about workers receiving benefits, he appeared surprised and shot back, "What benefits?" If most are unable to earn fringe benefits, what alternatives do temporary workers have? According to Johnson, "Temporary employees should set up their own retirement accounts and take out full insurance coverage for medical care and accidents."[15] However, it is highly unrealistic, given the prevailing low wages, that temporary workers could pursue this course. Later in her book Johnson acknowledged how ludicrous her own advice was when she noted, "Insurance premiums are sometimes the determining factor in turning temporary employees into permanent employees when they wish to receive company-paid benefit packages."[16] Aside from an occasional referral bonus, it would be presumptuous for temporary workers to expect to receive any fringe benefits. As Jamie Laughridge summarized, "For the most part, temps give up benefits, pensions, sick days and paid vacations. Some well-established services do have benefit programs, but they're generally offered only to those for whom temping is, in fact, a permanent job."[17]

Opportunities for Full-Time Employment

One benefit that may stem from being employed as a temporary worker is the opportunity to find full-time employment. The extent to which this occurs, however, is significantly overstated by the temporary help industry. For example, Kate Tomlin and Ron Kapche reported that 30 percent of temporary workers find permanent positions through temporary assignments.[18] An even more optimistic appraisal was offered by Roberts. To temporary employees seeking full-time jobs, she advised:

> As the time for your temporary placement draws to a close you will probably be asked directly whether or not you wish to remain with the organization. All the experts concur in the belief that if you've been on the job every day, have diligently performed your duties, shown initiative, been resourceful and achieved something, the company almost inevitably will evince a strong desire to recruit you to its permanent workforce.[19]

Among the temporary clerical workers interviewed for this book, only one reported being offered a full-time job, and she accepted.

The practice of temporary workers moving from contingent to permanent status is formally and informally discouraged. For example, virtually all temporary companies charge their clients a fee (usually $1,500) if the employer hires one of the company's temporary workers within ninety days of the initial assignment. As Edward Lenz noted, the purpose of charging "liquidated damages is to discourage customers from using the temporary help company as an employment agency—and a free one to boot."[20] An alternative arrangement that discourages temporary employees from becoming permanent workers is the requirement that employees remain on the temporary firm's account for a designated period (often thirteen weeks) after the date the worker has accepted the client's offer of employment. In addition, some temporary firms now require their employees to sign contracts with restrictive covenants. These agreements prohibit the employee from working for customers or competitors for a fixed period of time following the termination of employment. Perhaps of more profound importance than these formal obstacles is the resistance from employers, which is great because most are using temporary firms in an expanded way to avoid a commitment to additional full-time workers. As a Midwest management support supervisor stated in *The Office*, "We like the idea of temporary services, but we don't like it when temporaries begin feeling as if we should hire them after they have worked on several different long term assignments. Temporaries sometimes forget there are no obligations on our part to hire them full-time."[21]

The formal organizational structure of the temporary help industry does not facilitate or encourage its employees to make the transition from temporary to full-time work. Managers disagreed sharply over the frequency with which temporary workers moved into permanent employment. One manager said that as many as 30 to 40 percent of the firm's clerical employees eventually got full-time jobs with an employer for which they had worked previously as a temporary worker. A more commonly cited figure was 20 percent, and even that was an exaggeration. Most managers did not think in terms of all the temporary workers in their pool of available employees, just those working on a regular basis. Thus, the actual number of temporary workers moving from temporary to permanent employment appears to be quite negligible.

Skill Requirements

Temporary clerical workers are employed in a wide variety of working contexts. Some of them are challenging, requiring the use of considerable talent and skill. But among the temporary employees I met, the work was more frequently described as "boring," "stifling," "degrading," "dead-end," and "drudgery." The work may not be that disagreeable for highly trained technically oriented workers who exercise significant levels of discretion over their temporary assignments. But for less proficient clerical temps, boring, dead-end assignments are the norm.

One indication of the low skill level of temporary work is the pervasive sense of underutilization expressed by clerical employees. Of the workers interviewed for this book, approximately three-quarters expressed the belief that they were not fulfilling their potential employed as a temp. The following comments from workers about the nature of work assignments were typical:

"Anyone could do it."
"I'm overqualified for just about everything so far."
"None of the assignments were challenging."
"All of the work has been Mickey Mouse stuff."
"So far, everything I've done has been well beneath my capabilities."

A minority of workers said they felt their skills had been well utilized. Among these workers the prevailing view was that their lack of skill and training meant that no assignments were below their ability.

Temporary firm managers echoed this view in their comments. They readily acknowledged the low skill requirements of many assignments and the significant levels of underutilization among temporary workers. Some managers cited instances in which full-service secretaries filled a receptionist's job and word processing operators filled a clerk's position. In both cases the workers drew only minimally from their overall talent and training.

Generally managers have played down the level of underemployment among their employees, stressing instead companies' efforts to maximize the match between workers and assignments. In addition to the issue of underutilization, however, the use of temporary workers to perform boring work remains an important issue. Indeed, hiring temporary workers to handle boring work is a significant function for the clients of temporary companies. As intimated earlier, filling high-turnover positions (often boring ones) with temporary workers cuts labor costs and allows employers to keep morale high among full-time, permanent employees.

Learning New Skills

Another widespread myth about temporary employment is that it provides abundant opportunities for workers to learn new skills or upgrade existing ones. An executive with Adia Temporary Services remarked that "working at a temporary service is a practical, rapid means of acquiring or reacquiring skills needed to enter the job market. The temporary employee, by compressing 3–5 years of experience into a single year, achieves skill levels far ahead of comparable permanent employees."[22] Similarly, Johnson claimed that "as a temporary employee you may receive far more opportunities to learn new skills than most regular employees as you are exposed to different experiences and often learn new skills with nearly every new job. . . . Temporary work . . . can be one long process of continuing education."[23] It would be difficult to deliberately create more misleading information. Few temporary employees have any chance to learn or upgrade meaningful skills on the job.

Among the clerical workers, most reported that they had acquired no new skills while employed by a temporary firm. One responded to my query about obtaining skills this way: "The only thing I learned was that I didn't want to continue working as a temporary." There were some exceptions, however. One worker said she learned telemarketing skills, another employee acquired data-entry skills, still another learned several printing processes, and one worker discussed learning how to file. In addition, several workers said they acquired knowledge that was not directly skill related, such as insights about employers, good ole boy networks, and publicly supported assistance programs. Nevertheless, despite the protests of sympathetic observers, there is little evidence that the temporary help industry augments workers' skill levels.

Occupational Mobility

The skill-upgrading myth includes the notion that temporary workers are routinely assigned to varied and exciting occupations. For example, an executive with Victor Temporary Services stated, "Ambitious individuals can quickly improve income by acquiring new skills or upgrading existing ones."[24] A temporary help executive I interviewed extended the assertion that skill-driven mobility is greater for temporary workers than for full-time employees:

> Unlike permanent workers, office temporaries don't have to wait for a new job to open up within a single company to earn more money. Confronted with a variety of jobs, the temporary gains experience and more and better skills, which translate into more money. Because their jobs improve along with their skills, temporaries are less likely to become entrenched and frustrated.

I asked both workers and managers of temporary help firms about occupational mobility. I wanted to know if workers got better assignments or higher status and better-paying positions after a period as a temporary employee. Overall, about 20 percent of the clerical temps said they had experienced upward mobility since they had started working temporary assignments. For example, one clerical employee who worked "temporarily" for the same computer electronics firm for six consecutive months received a title upgrade, a raise in pay, and greater responsibilities while working for that firm. A clerical worker who made the transition from temporary to permanent employment also reported upward mobility. After six months she received the same package of fringe benefits as well as a greater measure of job security typically associated with full-time, permanent employment.

Overall, however, few clerical workers reported any advancement in their occupational standing. When I asked about mobility opportunities, most workers stated they did not view temporary employment in those terms. For some, mobility was never really considered: "You just take what you can, whatever is available." Others spoke of lateral mobility: "The jobs have been pretty much all the same," stated one clerical temp. Some associated occupational mobility in terms of aspects that had little to do with differences in occupational status. For instance, a receptionist spoke of improved assignments in terms of "staying busy" rather than objectively measurable improvements in working conditions.

Temporary workers have, at best, an ambiguous understanding of where they are located in the organizational hierarchy with respect to other employees working for the same firm. Once again uncertainty pierces the world of work for temporary employees. In most firms there is no internal labor market providing mobility opportunities for temporary workers. As the comments from managers suggest, the idea is to have a pool of workers similar enough in skill and talent that any "warm body" can be called at a moment's notice. This orientation is consistent with temporary help firms' primary allegiance to business clients as opposed to workers.

Managers of temporary help firms expressed a diverse set of views about worker mobility. At one end of the spectrum were managers who thought the whole issue of employees getting improved assignments was irrelevant and ludicrous. One simply laughed aloud when I broached the topic. Another manager responded:

> The question is inappropriate. . . . I may try to help the most qualified keep working, but this is to satisfy the clients. When a client calls, I have one-half hour to get someone to the job site. It may take one to six calls. Whoever I can get that matches the requirements is who I have to work with. I can't be concerned with helping workers advance.

Other managers were somewhat more sensitive about the issue of occupational mobility among their pool of temporary workers. Some managers indicated "individual initiative" and the acquisition of "higher-level skills" as attributes leading to better assignments. A few managers tied the issue to their firms' economic viability. One manager said any interest in helping workers improve their position stemmed from the company's immediate economic self-interest. This manager observed that occupational mobility was important because "higher skilled workers bring higher billing rates."

In the final analysis opportunities for better assignments are placed squarely on the workers' shoulders. Said one manager, "Occupational mobility depends on how much the worker desires. They can move up to better positions with greater pay and improved visibility." This manager provided the example of a typist who was promoted to personal computer operator after three months' continual employment as a common example of occupational mobility for temporary clerical workers.

Interaction with Permanent Workers

The presence or absence of permanent co-workers and the quality of interaction between the two are other aspects of temporary work life colored by uncertainty. For example, I always included "working with other workers" as a preference on my employment application. Despite that request, a majority of my clerical assignments involved isolated work settings. Most of the clerical employees I interviewed reported very little workplace interaction. Adjectives such as "polite" crept up frequently to characterize the interaction that did exist. The following comments from clerical workers were typical concerning workplace interaction:

- -"When you're there for a long period, you really get to know them and feel like you're part of the team. . . . On the other hand, if you are only there for a day or two, you don't feel like you really make much of a difference."
- -"There was hardly any interaction at all. Most of it was indifferent, just supervisors giving out instructions. . . . They tell you what to do and when to take breaks."
- -"People treat you nice and polite, but they also treat you differently. . . . There is no feeling of attachment, and sometimes attitudes are condescending."
- -"Overall, there was not much interaction. Most of the full-time people see a lot of faces come and go. They are interested in you getting the work done but don't want to know you personally. The emphasis is on casual relationships."
- -"Most of the interaction is characterized by uneasiness and ambiguity. . . . No one seems sure how to treat each other. I try to make an impression, but no one seems to care."
- -"Many people have been warm and extended themselves to me. But other assignments have been different. In some cases, the permanent workers seem to be threatened by the temps."
- -"The counselor at the service where I worked specifically told me never to talk with full-time employees."

This frequent lack of regular interaction with permanent workers has apparently contributed to the growing success of temporary help firms. In a brief review of the temporary help industry, the assistant editor of *Management World* stressed that "a temporary worker comes in fresh, alert, and ready to work, and is not socially or politically involved with other workers."[25] (Chapter 6 identifies the social and political noninvolvement of temporary employees in the workplace and the further subdivision of the workforce that this creates as one important function temporary workers provide for employers.)

Advantages of Temporary Employment

The temporary help industry aggressively markets a variety of alleged advantages of temporary work, including skill upgrading and flexible work schedules. During National Temporaries Week (an industry-sponsored promotional event), for example, the Canadian Federation of Temporary Help Services sponsors an essay contest for temporary employees to encourage them to write about their (positive) experiences as a temporary employee. According to *Temporary Topics*, "essay after essay told us that working temp provided needed employment (often as an entry or re-entry to the work force), helped develop skills, provided experience, allowed flexibility, and was an enjoyable change from routine."[26] One of the winners in the essay contest had high praise for temporary work. The essayist compared her "being in a rut" life in a permanent job to working as "a temp—a sort of rolling stone of the secretarial work force, not content to stay in one position gathering moss for more than a few weeks at a time." Of her learning experiences, this temporary clerical worker wrote, "I have learned how to make coffee in almost every coffee machine on the market. I can use manual, electric, and even electronic typewriters."[27]

Johnson identified several advantages that temporary employees may enjoy, including discretion over when and where to work, job satisfaction derived from working where they know they are really needed, fast pay for emergencies, prospects for finding permanent employment, opportunities to learn new skills, a chance to explore different types of jobs, and the likelihood of meeting new people.[28] Again, the evidence gathered for this book suggests that these advantages are difficult for workers to realize.

One survey of temporary workers conducted by Adia Temporary Services found that 44 percent listed the opportunity to broaden work experiences as the aspect of temporary employment they liked best. The canvass, which covered two thousand workers worldwide, also found that 44 percent considered variety of work and working hours as important advantages of temporary employment and that 42 percent identified flexibility as a major advantage.[29]

Gannon, in a mail survey of 1,101 temporary workers, found that only 16.6 percent cited variety as the most important reason for working as a temporary employee. In contrast, more than 60 percent chose freedom to schedule work in a flexible manner as the most important reason for electing a contingent work arrangement.[30] In my interviews, these advantages were mentioned, but typically they had a different spin. Here is how a few of the clerical employees expressed the advantages of temporary work:

-"I like meeting different people."
-"The flexibility, not having to work every day . . . getting away from the monotonous drag of everyday work."
-"You can sort of be irresponsible in that if they call you for a job, you don't have to go, only if you feel like it."
-"The idea that you could work whenever you want and be off whenever you want."
-"Getting paid on a weekly basis."
-"You can quit anytime you want; you don't feel obligated to any single employer."
-"The opportunities for leisure . . . You can leave a job you hate. . . . The variety of work experiences."
-"I didn't like anything about being a temp; it was just a way to pay bills."

Several themes emerge in these and similar comments made by temporary clerical workers. The first is that the flexibility touted by the temporary help industry is a double-edged sword: flexibility accrues advantages for temporary firms and employers but fails to consistently benefit temporary workers. Clearly, employers and the temporary help industry gain inordinately from a flexible workforce. As Karen Nussbaum of the National Association of Working Women

(9 to 5) suggested, the benefit of flexibility is extended on management's terms.[31] For temporary employees the chance to schedule work in a flexible manner is a limited benefit at best.

Another theme revealed in these comments is that flexibility, variety, and the other advantages cited by workers are frequently couched in a kind of tentative, hesitant language. Indeed, many workers seemed to have had a difficult time identifying any advantages. When conducting in-depth interviews, I probed on flexibility and variety (the advantages most frequently cited by industry and worker surveys). Despite the probes, neither feature emerged as a significant theme in the workers' comments concerning advantages. Indeed, few workers openly identified variety and flexibility as advantages of temporary work. Other workers cast the advantages in plainly negative terms. To illustrate, consider the worker who said, "You can quit anytime you want." This employee is intimating something quite different about temporary work from one who says that working as a temporary employee offers variety and the opportunity to learn new things. Similarly, the statement that "you can leave a job you hate" is not conveying anything positive about temporary employment. It is merely expressing the somewhat dubious benefit of being able to choose between idling oneself indefinitely or being subjected to unpleasant working conditions. It is the kind of advantage that is mentioned only after other, more common advantages, such as adequate pay and job security, have been eliminated.

Few temporary clerical workers identified advantages of temporary work that could be labeled outwardly and explicitly positive. Among temporary workers the prevailing sentiment was that it was advantageous to work for a temporary help firm because they could quickly leave disagreeable working conditions. In this sense temporary work becomes an advantageous arrangement because it means a worker can leave offensive workplaces without permanent termination.

Managers emphasized more conventional connotations surrounding flexibility as a major advantage for temporary workers. According to firm executives, workers desire flexibility in order to have a family life and a work life or to continue an education. Additionally, managers frequently cited variety and the opportunity to earn cash quickly as advantages. Several were candid in acknowledging that there were few genuine advantages associated with a temporary working arrangement. One executive prefaced her remarks about the advantages of working as a temporary employee this way:

> Temporary work is not good for everyone and is not to be recommended to just anyone. It's no way to make a living because even if you sign up with every outfit in town, there will be days without work. Then there is the lack of benefits. So the advantages here are for those individuals who have self-selected themselves for this kind of schedule.

Another manager said a major advantage is that because of ever-changing work sites, a temporary worker is "less likely to get bored or burnt out." Contained here is a highly qualified view of the advantages of temporary work. The managers' views do not overtly convey anything intrinsically positive about temporary work. Rather, the benefits can be more accurately characterized as workers' rational reactions to the dead-end, demoralizing character of so much full-time employment in the U.S. economy.

There is, however, an important alternative interpretation of the advantages identified by temporary employees. It could be argued that temporary workers are reasserting control over their working lives through the use of temporary help companies. When workers turn down an offer of employment, they are sending a signal about the perceived quality of the work. Temporary help firms offer an unusual opportunity for (regularly employed) temporary workers to determine an important aspect of their working lives: when and how often they will work.

Nonetheless, the attempt to recover a portion of their alienated labor may be of only marginal significance. When temporary workers do decide to begin accepting assignments again, they are relegated to the bottom of the occupational hierarchy. Furthermore, when temporary employees remain idle, they are seldom eligible for unemployment compensation or paid days off. Full-time workers, in contrast, can occasionally take off for a "mental health day" at their employer's expense.

The benefits of being employed as a temporary worker are limited. To workers they are advantages because the world of full-time employment seems even more dreary, monotonous, and dismal.

These peculiarly qualified advantages reflect the alienation that both permanent and temporary workers experience under U.S. capitalism. Perhaps to justify working under an arrangement that offers so few visible benefits, some temporary workers "find" advantages in their jobs even where few exist.

Disadvantages of Temporary Employment

According to both workers and managers of temporary firms, the disadvantages of being employed as a temporary clerical worker far outdistance the benefits. As this chapter closes, I return to the fundamental issue of the uncertainty that burdens temporary workers. Nearly all the temporary workers identified insecurity as the underlying problem of being employed on a temporary basis. Temporary workers routinely face uncertainty regarding when they will work, the length of their assignments, and the quality of co-worker and supervisory interaction, not to mention the numerous daily nuances in organizational procedures.

Beyond this insecurity and uncertainty (called flexibility by employers and the temporary help industry), temporary employees mentioned other aspects of temporary employment they disliked. The following excerpted comments are representative of the disadvantages typically voiced by temporary clerical workers:

- -"doing the same thing all the time . . . it's bad and boring work."
- -"When you are sent out to a job, a lot of people look down on you. They think that temporaries are very unskilled or poor people. . . . It's not always true."
- -"The constant adjustment to new faces and the untried job routine. Being held in low esteem because of temporary status is a big problem . . . the perception that 'temporary' is a category that is okay to discriminate against."
- -"I didn't like the often antagonistic attitude of the regular workers toward me and the other temps. We were looked down upon because we were 'just temps.'"
- -"My problem was the gap between the projected image of the service and the reality of the assignments. They made it sound

as if you could work any time you wanted. . . . They also made it sound like there was a lot of different work to do. But it looks like it's all dead-end work you couldn't stand to do for more than one day."

-"The uncertainty . . . never knowing when and how much work there will be."

-"You only get paid if you work . . . no holiday or vacation pay. I didn't like getting an assignment for one week and then being asked to leave before the time was up. I also didn't like the hectic pace of much of the work."

-"It's stifling work, completely without content. One big problem is that you never get to complete a job; you've got several bosses and they are always switching you around."

Several central issues surrounding temporary employment emerge in these comments. One distinct problem is the absence of varied and interesting assignments. This disadvantage stands in direct contrast to the industry's position that temporary work offers employees a great diversity of occupations to fill. Actually, workers are employed in many different industries, but as several employees suggested, this means "doing the same thing all of the time." If a worker performs data-entry work, the tasks are quite similar despite dissimilar industrial contexts. And again these comments raise the issue of everyday uncertainty. One worker referred to the "constant adjustment to new faces"; another echoed a common complaint about "never knowing when you're going to work."

Beyond these negative aspects, a prominent issue was the stigma associated with working as a temporary employee. Temporary workers repeatedly expressed the feeling of being shunned because they were not permanent workers. The popular phrase workers used to describe themselves and other temporary workers was "warm bodies." In similar fashion the workers labeled the temporary companies "flesh peddlers." Temps found they were not treated like other workers; because of their contingent status, they did not command the same level of respect as full-time workers. There were, of course, some temporary clerical workers who expressed no complaints. Said one, "Nothing bothered me. . . . I didn't need the income, so pay wasn't an issue." But overall, with little probing, the majority expressed a profound underside connected with temporary employment.

This devalued view of temporary workers is held by many co-workers. That many accept the impression that these workers are *"just* temps" appears to stem from the occupations they most commonly occupy. Temporary workers serve many different roles, labor at a wide range of jobs, but usually make major sacrifices in every important occupational dimension related to job satisfaction. They are paid less; receive few, if any, fringe benefits; and are assigned the most mundane jobs within organizations. For managers and full-time co-workers, temporary and other contingent employees represent a new substratum of workers.

Conclusion

The majority of temporary clerical workers are full-time job seekers who have exhausted alternative working arrangements. By and large the managers of temporary firms acknowledged that the disadvantages outlined here involve serious workplace problems. The issue of unsteady, irregular, and uncertain employment was identified by all but one of the temporary managers as the central disadvantage of temporary clerical work.

In the following chapter, I turn to an inside look at temporary industrial work. So-called light industrial workers share much in common with the temporary clerical workforce. Temporary industrial workers are fewer in number than clerical workers but in some ways experience the adversity of temporary employment at a more extreme level. Together these two examples of temporary workers provide us with a representative look at the work life created by the burgeoning temporary help industry.

5

TEMPORARY INDUSTRIAL WORKERS

FROM THE WORKERS' perspective, there are few meaningful differences between temporary clerical and temporary industrial work. In particular, the omnipresent uncertainty of temporary work is as much an everyday reality for light industrial workers as it is for clerical employees. Indeed, in some respects the uncertainty surrounding temporary work is exacerbated for light industrial employees. More of them, for example, complained about the unavailability of steady employment than did clerical workers. Also, industrial workers cited a far wider range of daily working environments to which they had to adapt rapidly than did clerical workers. But like temporary clerical workers, industrial temps tend to be full-time job seekers. And like involuntary part-time workers, subcontracted workers, and others in the contingent workforce, temporary industrial workers share an underemployed status in the labor force, enduring uncertain hours, inadequate income, and a fundamental mismatch between their skills and the opportunities afforded by the temporary help industry.

Although still substantial, the portion of the temporary help industry devoted to providing industrial workers is declining. In 1986, 16 percent of workers were classified as industrial workers. By 1990, the percentage had slipped to 14.8 percent.[1] Within the industry this percentage loss has been made up in the technical and medical sectors. Reflecting the broader transformation in the U.S. economy toward a service base, the industrial sector has dwindled in significance. Nonetheless, most temporary help firms retain a light industrial division along with a clerical section.

Type of Work

In contrast to temporary clerical employees, who customarily are assigned to work in air-conditioned offices, the typical light industrial worker frequently labors in a variety of harsh, unprotected, and unpredictable environments. A quintessential temporary assignment for industrial employees is a stint in a warehouse. Other types of assignments also involve manual labor, including preparing and cleaning up construction sites, loading and unloading trucks, hauling trash, filling security and surveillance positions, delivering and installing appliances, stocking shelves, performing assembly and manufacturing work, moving furniture, doing landscaping, performing lumberyard work, installing insulation, cutting tile, maintaining physical plants, binding books, stringing cable, maintaining grounds, and doing inventory work. Despite this diversity, assignments involving warehouse and delivery work were mentioned far more frequently than other positions by temporary employees.

A Day in the Life of a Light Industrial Worker

I completed several light industrial assignments during my time as a temporary worker. Consistent with the reported experiences of industrial temps who agreed to in-depth interviews, the majority of my assignments involved warehouse work. The following is a brief account of an assignment I completed for a major retailing chain while employed as a temporary worker.

On the morning of the assignment, I phoned the temporary company's office at approximately 7:20 A.M. to check on work availability. The firm's job dispatcher said there would be no assignments available for me that day. About twenty minutes later, however, she called back with an offer for a light industrial assignment. This quick turnaround of circumstances illustrates both the uncertainty surrounding the availability of work and the short notice commonly given to and expected of temporary employees. Taking note of the employer's address and other details, I accepted the temporary firm's offer and headed for the warehouse.

On this assignment I had been hired by a major U.S. retailer that needed so-called special-project workers. The retail company's regional management was attempting to reorganize a local warehouse more efficiently. In addition to myself, more than a dozen other temporary workers were assigned for this special project. I later learned that I had been called in as a last-minute replacement for a temporary employee who, according to another worker's account, decided that yet another mid-August day in a warehouse was intolerable. His reluctance to return was easy enough to comprehend; by the time I arrived at 8:30 A.M., the temperature had surpassed ninety degrees.

The job site on this occasion was easy to find, but the pervasive uncertainty that characterizes temporary employment was evident in my inability to locate the appropriate personnel upon arriving. Furthermore, the temporary company that had arranged the assignment did not know to whom I should report. For roughly ten minutes I toured the inside of the warehouse before finding the supervisor. After being introduced to the first of several managers from whom I would take instructions that day, I began my day-long task—rotating appliances from one part of the warehouse to another. At first I moved water softeners, then tool kits, and later drill presses, but it was all the same kind of manual work.

Despite the mundane activity, this assignment was particularly valuable to me in terms of understanding light industrial temporary employment from the workers' perspective. It allowed me to interact informally with as many as twelve other temporary workers at one time. In addition, it eventually yielded several in-depth interviews. One of the interviews that stemmed from this assignment was with Ron, a recently divorced, black Vietnam veteran. Compared with most temporary employees I met, Ron displayed a significant level of assertiveness at the workplace. For example, he remarked to one of our supervisors that "we don't need any of your help" (in organizing the warehouse). Also on this assignment, I worked alongside, and interviewed, Tim, a white thirty-two-year-old who had recently quit working as a drummer for a local band. Another light industrial temp in my immediate work group was Tom, a white forty-year-old who had recently been operating a small engraving shop in the central city. The four of us had lunch at my house that day and became better acquainted.

Back on the job that afternoon, rotating stock grew increasingly disagreeable, difficult, and dangerous as the temperature eventually climbed to 103 degrees. Much of the work we had earlier accomplished solely with our backs was increasingly relegated to forklifts and dollies. In midafternoon, as a collective expression of our discomfort, we took a half-hour break, a period three times longer than officially allowed. When we returned to work, one manager began to convey his disapproval about the time our idleness had consumed. Before he could finish, however, he was cut off by Ron, who relayed his own displeasure about this particular supervisor's "rigid" managerial approach. Given the heat and arduous labor, none of the temps expressed feeling particularly guilty about slowing the work pace or taking extra time off. Even the head supervisor was sympathetic. And despite our transgression, the retailer's management encouraged all of us to return the following day.

After the late afternoon break, we were instructed to perform tasks typically forbidden by temporary help firms. Specifically, the work involved disassembling two sections of scaffolding that rose more than thirty feet. All the storage components were made of long, awkward, heavy pieces of metal and required at least two workers to handle them safely. Accomplishing this task genuinely aroused concerns within me about safety, especially because of the lateness of the day and the fact that the work required all the stamina and alertness that could be mustered. Nonetheless, we successfully completed the last-minute chore without incident, signed out, and left for home by 5:00 P.M.

Two general points are noteworthy about this temporary assignment. First, the work itself was dead-end, offering no opportunities to learn new skills or hone existing ones. With the exception of operating a forklift, the work required no formal skills and no ongoing supervisory instruction or on-the-job training. Several co-workers that day expressed the belief that temporary employees are often assigned dead-end work because permanent employees cannot handle its stifling character.

Second, there were several modes of worker resistance that temporary employees exercised to protest the numbing assignments. As intimated earlier, temporary workers have several methods at their disposal to resist the exploitative working conditions they encounter. The most fundamental form is to simply resign from temporary work arrangements or routinely decline assignments when temporary firms make an offer. This is not a practical strategy, however, since most temporary employees are working out of economic necessity. Another form of worker resistance I witnessed was the deliberate restriction of output. At the warehouse assignment workers cajoled one another not to give more than $4.00 an hour worth of effort (the wage they were being paid that day). Taking frequent breaks is yet another method. On the warehouse assignment described here, workers left early for lunch, extended allotted breaks beyond specified time limits, and took numerous other informal breaks. When resistance surfaced, temporary workers often discussed the issue and justified their behavior in terms of the lack of employer commitment and the generally dubious working conditions they confronted.

From the temporary firm's perspective, the most problematic form of resistance is a practice known as "walking"—in which a worker leaves before the assignment is complete. Temporary help companies would prefer workers decline an assignment when offered rather than leave before one is finished. I witnessed one light industrial worker walking off the job and heard about the practice from employees, managers, and employers. Of the three temporary co-workers I worked closely with at the warehouse, two had walked. One left a lumberyard because he felt the management there was acting arbitrarily. Another walked off alleging bigoted supervision. On yet another occasion an employee I was working with walked off the job; referring to the filing task we had been assigned, he simply said, "I've had enough of this" and exited.

The employees at the retailer's warehouse also intimated that pilferage and sabotage were ways workers could avenge circumstances they perceived as unfair. One sign of this approach was the casual disregard workers showed for the employer's inventory while they were rotating stock. But these latter forms of worker resistance may be more talk than substance. Despite the low pay and often demanding labor, the industrial employees I worked with demonstrated a high level of attachment to work in general and to working hard on a daily basis. In short, there are several ways that temporary workers can, and do, exhibit their dissatisfaction with their contingent employment arrangement; some, such as turning down or walking off selected jobs, are fairly specific to temporary employees, whereas others, such as sabotage and restriction of output, are practiced by workers everywhere.[2]

Indicators of Marginal Status

Skill Underutilization

As the preceding vignette highlights, much of the work assigned to industrial temporary workers lacks meaningful content. When asked, a majority of the industrial temps replied that no skills or training was required for the work they were assigned. A minority reported that an insignificant amount of skill or training was required. The following statements concerning skill requirements are taken from in-depth interviews and are representative of the comments I collected from industrial workers:

- -"The only requirement is the ability to move boxes around all day."
- -"You have to have a phone, a car, and the ability to speak English. You can't have any physical ailments or disabilities."
- -"There are no skills or training required, just plenty of muscle."
- -"There is little skill required; a tenth grade education would suffice."
- -"The work just takes common sense and the ability to follow directions."
- -"The only thing that is required is a willingness to work."

The main message these comments convey is that the majority of work performed by temporary employees requires few, if any, skills.

Temporary industrial workers are not required to perform work that challenges them or exerts great demands in terms of skill or intelligence. The only real requirements are a willingness to follow directions unquestioningly and to perform physically demanding manual labor.

With the exception of electronics assembly workers (who must know how to solder), managers of temporary firms largely affirmed the view that most assignments involve unskilled labor. When asked about opportunities to learn new skills on the job, few industrial temps could identify any. One worker who was making the transition from a temporary to a permanent position with a large electronics firm did learn marketable maintenance skills, such as plumbing and electrical wiring. In addition, like clerical temps, some industrial temporary employees reported acquiring knowledge that was not directly skill related. For example, one "learned what dead-end zombielike jobs most people have." Another talked about learning from the inside "about the waste and inefficiency that exist in many bureaucratic organizations." And one worker said that the diversity of working environments and personalities "impressed upon me the importance of learning to get along."

Because industrial employees acquire few skills on the job, many believed they were underutilized on their temporary assignments, although a small number did maintain that temporary assignments adequately used their training, skills, and talents. Among those who said they were underutilized, most said they felt that way during most of their assignments. Several workers identified specific skills or talents they possessed but never had a chance to use, such as welding and building maintenance skills. Others spoke of the work experience gained from the armed services, time in college, or full-time jobs that they had expected to use working as a temporary employees. With respect to skill underutilization, one industrial temp succinctly summed up the issue, observing, "The work has never been a challenge in the skill or intelligence area. They do, however, make full utilization of you from the moment you arrive. . . . Most employers have the full day mapped out for you, but there is no thinking involved."

As was true of the twenty temporary clerical workers with whom I conducted in-depth interviews, virtually all the industrial employees had previous full-time working experience. Their work history spanned a wide range of occupations. Previous vocations included schoolteachers, food service workers, military personnel, salespersons, maintenance workers, electronics assemblers, bartenders, construction workers, journalists, and tow-truck drivers. This diversity and the extent of full-time working experience among industrial employees are at odds with the industry-promoted notion that temporary workers are new entrants to the labor force or that they seek temporary employment to maximize leisure time. Much of their previous work experience included the use of skills that remain marketable in many industries and regions.

When asked about their preferences, only 20 percent of the industrial workers expressly wanted a temporary employment arrangement. The remaining workers urgently wanted to be working on a permanent or a full-time basis. Of those who reported preferring temporary employment, half were full-time schoolteachers waiting to return to their permanent positions. Two others had permanent part-time jobs that consumed twenty-five hours weekly. All the workers without full-time jobs indicated a first preference for being employed on a permanent basis. The reasons provided by the temporary industrial workers cited for preferring full-time work were predictable enough. Said one, "I prefer the security and stability of full-time employment. I don't especially relish working for someone different every day. . . . I also miss the benefits." Another added, "When you have a full-time job, you know you have a job; you can count on working."

Some of the industrial workers who preferred full-time employment argued that working temporary assignments interfered with full-time job hunting. This view had also been articulated by the clerical temps. Because of the uncertainty associated with their work schedules, temporary employees never know when an assignment will conflict with a job interview or an important phone call from a potential permanent employer.

An examination of their future expectations also suggests that industrial temporary workers bear an involuntary, underemployed status. For example, when asked how long they expected to continue working as a temporary employee, the consensus response was "until full-time work is found." Few workers had a concrete idea of how long that would take. One industrial employee who had been working temporary assignments for three months expressed surprise with himself for staying with it as long as he had. When asked about the kind of occupation they expected to have in the future, most provided responses characteristic of full-time workers with a strong attachment to the labor force. As many job satisfaction surveys have revealed, many workers expect to be "self-employed" in the future. Industrial temps are no exception. Others expected to be musicians, computer workers, construction workers, managers, food caterers, or simply "professionals." Only one expected to be working at an occupation remotely similar to the one he had been performing as a temporary employee.

As with the temporary clerical workforce, most of the temporary industrial workers applied for temporary work after exhausting more desirable alternatives. For the schoolteachers, it filled a three-month shortfall in their permanent employment. For several others it was a matter of having recently arrived to an area and needing a source of quick income. Still others applied with temporary help firms after being laid off or quitting their most recent full-time job. Thus, in both their previous labor force experiences and in their future expectations, temporary workers are oriented toward the world of permanent full-time employment. None of these workers indicated a primary attachment to any domain of life other than work. Among their number could be found no leisure seekers, or students.

Adequacy of Hours

Most industrial workers appear, then, to be full-time job seekers who are ready and willing to accept permanent positions when available. Predictably, temporary industrial workers attempt to work as many hours each week as possible. Over the short term most of them report being relatively satisfied with the amount of hours worked. Again, a minority said they were not working, on average, an adequate number of hours. Among the traditional dimensions of marginal labor market status, adequacy of hours worked is the only indicator where temporary workers, by their own accounting, are not clearly underemployed. This is true despite the fact that few industrial employees regularly work full-time schedules. Only a handful of industrial temps who were satisfied with the amount of work they were assigned regularly completed, on average, forty-hour workweeks. Some temporary employees who said they were satisfied with their hours were working as little as eight hours weekly. Of the remaining employees, average hours worked weekly ranged from sixteen to thirty-five. One worker said there was too much variation from week to week to provide an answer.

As a group the industrial employees reported that three days was the norm for a temporary assignment. Virtually all had experienced working a partial day, often involving construction cleanup work or truck loading or unloading. The longest assignment reported by any of the temporary industrial workers interviewed for this book was sixteen months. Only two had worked for one employer for as long as two weeks. Managers of temporary firms indicated the typical assignment for industrial workers tended to be shorter than the thirty-two hour average cited for clerical workers.

Like temporary clerical workers, light industrial employees share much in common with involuntary part-time workers, subcontracted workers, and other divisions of the contingent workforce. Despite the fact that many are satisfied with the amount of hours worked during particular weeks, these industrial workers are not working as temporary employees voluntarily; they are working for the temporary help industry because of tight labor market conditions in general and because of slack demand for their skills in particular.

Advantages of Temporary Work

The advantages identified by the temporary industrial workers echoed those articulated by the clerical temps. According to temporary industrial workers, variety and flexibility are the two most important advantages of temporary work. The opportunity to earn cash quickly was mentioned frequently, as was the chance to meet people. Here is how a sample of industrial workers expressed the advantages of temporary employment:

-"You don't have to work at a job you don't like, except for maybe one day. And then you go to another job."

-"The fact that if you don't feel like working one day, you don't
have to. Of course, if you turn down a service even once, it
pisses them off."
-"Freedom is the most important thing . . . the freedom to work
when you want for as long as you want. You're not obligated to
anyone. . . . It's convenient; you do it when you want to."
-"I like the flexibility involved; I can take time off for school, vacation, or for any other reason that might come up."
-"The best thing is knowing you don't have to come back. . . . A
bad job doesn't have to last forever. I also like working somewhere where you know you are really needed."
-"The camaraderie among the temps was one of the best things. I
felt there was a real sense of pulling together and chipping in to
get the job done."
-"Since you're not attached to the customer, there is no pressure to
excel."

In these comments and others, several themes about temporary
work emerge. As with the orientation of temporary clerical workers,
the aspect of temporary work that industrial workers value most is
the opportunity to decline jobs they believe are unsatisfying. Once
again the chief benefits of temporary work are couched in a peculiarly negative language.

These industrial employees are not expressing how gratifying it is
to be working on a temporary schedule or how intrinsically rewarding they find the work. Rather, they are championing their ability to
avoid working under unfavorable conditions. These employees are
not even saying that temporary work provides more leisure time,
merely that it gives them the chance to avoid undesirable jobs. In
short, temporary industrial workers report the greatest advantage of
temporary work is the ability to selectively choose work assignments
based on how attractive or unattractive they appear. The industry
hyperbole, that temping offers workers abundant opportunities for
skill upgrading and mobility from temporary to permanent jobs,
stands in sharp contrast to the reported experiences of many
workers.

Beyond this industry-oriented version of flexibility, the industrial
employees' comments did uncover some genuine advantages of

temporary working arrangements. One was the chance to meet people. Several industrial employees reported pleasant interaction with other workers. One temporary employee remarked, "Most of the interaction with other workers was positive; they treated me real nice." Another added that "relations were usually pretty good. . . . I was surprised to find how easy it was to walk in and get acquainted." Other temporary employees corroborated these sentiments.

Another industrial worker, after working on a temporary basis with an electronics firm for an extended period, was offered full-time employment, complete with fringe benefits. Two workers who had full-time positions as schoolteachers cited as advantageous the convenience of working on a temporary basis during the summer, simply reactivating their files each year. Others cited "working outdoors," "weekly paychecks," and "minimal bureaucratic interference" as advantages of working for a temporary help company.

From the workers' perspective, then, there are a number of advantages to temporary employment. For most temporary industrial employees, however, the disadvantages clearly outweigh the advantages. Very few workers receive the fringe benefits traditionally associated with full-time employment. Indeed, only 15 percent of the workers who agreed to in-depth interviews reported receiving *any* type of benefit. One worker received workers' compensation payments when an iron rod fell on his wrist while he was moving stock at a lumberyard. Another employee, the only industrial worker in this study who made the transition from temporary to permanent status, earned vacation pay, holiday pay, and bonuses for referring other workers. One other worker also earned a referral bonus.

Disadvantages of Temporary Work

The comments made by temporary employees about workplace interaction were not uniformly positive. Evoking a different, less collegial image of interpersonal interaction are the following comments:

- "They are nice to you if you bust your butt because they expect so little of you in the first place. They expect the worst and are pleasantly surprised at a good worker."

-"There is not much interaction at all. . . . Most of it has been routine and indifferent, people just going through the motions."

-"There is not a lot of interaction with other regular workers, just with supervisors mostly. What interaction exists tends to be negative. . . . It's the low-level character of the work. Temps are laborers doing the jobs nobody else would take."

-"I don't see much interaction with other workers; most of them just ignore you. They know you're not going to be there long. Some try to boss you around like you are the lowest thing around."

-"There seems to be mostly negative to indifferent interaction with the full-time workers. The bosses are glad to see you; they're happy to have you there. And there is camaraderie among the temps, but mostly indifference from the permanent employees."

-"Most of the time the regular workers are glad to have you around; they know you're there to clean up a mess, usually of their making. Sometimes you get assholes who have to act like big shots."

-"Most of the permanent workers treat you like you're just passing through; you're not attached to them in any way. . . . They just ignore you."

Although the workers cited earlier could identify a sense of camaraderie as an advantage associated with temporary employment, most industrial temps are more ambivalent about their workplace interaction. These comments highlight some of the salient characteristics of what it means to be a temporary worker. One important element is the all-encompassing sense of being resigned to the very bottom of the employer's workforce regardless of the assignment. Many of the temporary industrial workers found disconcerting the reality that even the lowest-ranking permanent worker in an organization was in a superordinate position over them. The interpersonal indifference that awaits many temporary workers on their assignments is another theme that emerges from worker interviews. Full-time co-workers recognize that temporary employees are routinely shuffled in and out, so few find it worth their time to become personally involved in any particular temp. That may explain why the worker camaraderie just mentioned referred to an esprit de corps among temporary employees rather than among the entire workforce.

With one exception, the industrial temps I interviewed expressed no reluctance in identifying aspects they liked least about temporary work. Along with predictable complaints about low pay, lack of benefits, and dead-end work, several industrial workers cited the stigma attached to their status as a significant drawback of working as a temp. The following comments further characterize the more disagreeable aspects of work life for industrial temps:

- -"The subhuman expectations of employers—we're just warm bodies. No one expects us to think or have feelings."
- -"Never knowing who your boss is going to be—I've really enjoyed some supervisors, but others seem indifferent or otherwise difficult to work with. I don't like the stigma that comes with being a temp. The permanent workers act as if they expect zero output from you. . . . They expect the worst."
- -"The unstable pattern of working life—some days you're without work, and other days they want you there at 7:00 A.M. . . . It's hard to stay in a routine that way. I also felt some shame about being a temp. Since my parents are both professional workers, it just seemed like a real step down for me to be doing this."
- -"Every time I really need or want to work, they don't seem to have enough for me. I also don't like the physical character of most of the 'light' industrial labor."
- -"Being treated like a slave by temporary employers—they have minimal expectations about the abilities of temps and their skills."

The issue of being labeled "just a temp" or a "warm body" was less pronounced among clerical temporary workers than among industrial employees. Many industrial workers clearly believed they had been singled out for differential, negative treatment because of their temporary status, that they were devalued by employers and permanent co-workers. Beyond the ignominious status of being a warm body, several industrial employees said low pay was the aspect they objected to most about temporary work. Most industrial temporary employees are low-wage workers. Only 15 percent of the ones interviewed for this book averaged as much as $5.00 an hour. The most frequently cited wage was $4.50 an hour, with $3.65 representing the low end and $5.00 the top. One temporary industrial worker refused to comment about pay. Other principal complaints listed by industrial employees were unsteady work, inadequate hours, lack of benefits, and overall uncertainty related to temporary schedules. Finally, several workers' greatest objection to temporary employment was its consistent failure to provide opportunities to fully utilize their skills and training.

Health, Safety, and Temporary Work

Contingent clerical workers face the same workplace hazards as full-time clerical workers, such as eye strain, headaches, and exposure to airborne pollution from ventilation systems. Similarly, temporary industrial workers find that their manual labor assignments often mirror the hazards confronted by their permanent counterparts. But because of the uncertainty of temporary working arrangements, the potential for industrial temps to be injured may be higher than their full-time counterparts. The working conditions of industrial temps typically range from uncomfortable to dangerous.

One industrial assignment I fulfilled for a temporary help company will illustrate some of the typical hazards encountered by temporary employees. Other assignments will illustrate the extra potential for harm deriving from temporary work. This particular assignment was for an appliance company. The main task that day was similar to the one described earlier—rotating and organizing warehouse stock. On this hot summer day the temperature peaked at ninety-eight degrees, but in the mostly enclosed warehouse, it seemed much warmer. Indeed, as a co-worker and I ascended the shelving units that held the appliances, we could sense the temperature climbing appreciably. Being romoved from any liquid refreshment compounded the discomfort wrought by the afternoon heat. There were no drinking fountains or vending machines available. The only water anywhere was lukewarm and came from the bathroom sink. My co-worker (also a temporary employee) and I were unsupervised in the afternoon; no one was there to give us a break so that we could get something to drink. After two and one-half hours, my energy level was at a low ebb, and I felt generally depleted.

When our supervisor returned, I asked if he had brought anything to drink. He replied, "A Dr. Pepper," which he then quickly consumed. After expressing my chagrin at his blatant lack of concern about our welfare, he offered us the company truck, which we used to search for the nearest convenience store. The lack of drinking water, although atypical, was nonetheless consistent with the pervasive uncertainty surrounding workplace conditions faced by temporary industrial workers.

In addition to heat-related discomfort, warehouse jobs pose other potential hazards. One way that temporary work can become more hazardous than the same work performed by full-time employees is when workers are not used to working and coordinating tasks with one another. One commonly encountered threat was the precarious manner in which heavy appliances were stored. On two warehouse assignments I worked, the stock was physically configured using hand dollies and forklifts. Danger often arises in such situations when stock is being transferred from the forklift to the shelving area. At that moment workers have little room to secure their footing while switching from the lift to the storage units. At the appliance warehouse my temporary co-worker, despite having an outwardly strong physical appearance, expressed great concern about the process. During the previous day, he had "felt certain there was going to be an accident" as he and another employee had wrestled with heavy appliances twenty-five to thirty feet in the air atop the forklift.

Another type of occupational hazard found in these light industrial assignments are various complications stemming from the physically demanding nature of the jobs. Such problems include strains, bruises, pulled muscles, and fatigue. A light industrial assignment I completed for a public-sector employer illustrates how lingering physical maladies can occur. Like other assignments, this one was punctuated by uncertainty surrounding parking, specific work tasks, supervisors, and working conditions. But along with these usual sources of uncertainty came several situations conducive to workplace injuries.

Many of the problems noted here are faced by all industrial workers. With temporary employees, however, potential problems are magnified by working alongside unfamiliar co-workers and supervisors and working in the unfamiliar physical layout of the employer's workplace. For example, because the workplace is unfamiliar, temporary employees must exercise greater caution to avoid everyday safety problems that permanent workers negotiate unconsciously. Steps that appear suddenly and blind spots in hallways are two common hazards. Furthermore, because the workers are unfamiliar with one another, their effort is less coordinated than would be the case among a group of full-time workers. And because of the short duration of assignments, permanent workers are less likely to be associated with, and committed to, the welfare of temporary employees. Unfamiliarity with supervision adds a further element of ambiguity that enhances the possibility of workplace injuries.

Several points related to work hazards can be gleaned from this public-sector assignment. Before I went to the work site, the temporary company's dispatcher had merely instructed me that the work would involve "moving some files around." This assignment had sounded straightforward, but the task was considerably more problematic. Simply put, the filing cabinets were among the largest, heaviest, and most awkward that I had ever seen. Standing alone, they were roughly five feet wide and eight feet high. Each cabinet contained forty letter-sized filing drawers. And each of the individual drawers was stuffed with police warrants for various offenses. A co-worker (also a temporary employee) and I were instructed to move six of these filing cabinets from one area in the building to another space approximately thirty yards away. Without being introduced to each other, my co-worker and I began sliding the first oversized cabinet onto the dolly. When my co-worker appeared reluctant, I took the initiative, pulling the dolly back in order to haul the cabinet away. When I pulled, the weight of the cabinet caused it to lurch, hitting my shoulders and upper arms. For several days afterward the vestiges of this momentary impact lingered.

My co-worker was of little assistance, merely guiding the cabinet after I had finished the more arduous part. As it turned out, however, he had a legitimate reason for being cautious. He said he was hampered by a form of muscular dystrophy and was recovering from a related shoulder dislocation. This employee, who also admitted to being a recovering opiate addict, had explicitly informed the temporary firms that he did not want to be assigned positions involving any heavy work. Frustrated with the physically demanding nature of the work, he walked. This working context, which was described by temporary firm managers as not uncommon, clearly involved unpredictable and dangerous work.

The warehouse assignment described at some length at the beginning of this chapter also presented a number of health and safety hazards. In particular, the disassembly of the steel storage units involved climbing between twenty and thirty feet and working above our heads. The scaffolding that held the shelving was heavy and required the concerted attention of at least two workers. Then there was the combined effect of heavy manual work and temperatures of one hundred degrees or more. Many industrial employees expressed concerns about the potential for heat-related problems when asked about working conditions. Said one, "Heat exhaustion and heat stroke are real threats. . . . moving stock around and going from hot to cold and back all day can get to you."

Even though permanent employees perform the same work as temporary workers, the former are more likely to be covered by group health insurance programs. With the potential for work-related injuries being frequently exacerbated for temporary employees, the dilemma of being both injured and unprotected by insurance becomes that much greater.

When workers were asked if they had ever been sent on an assignment they considered dangerous or unhealthy, several other potential workplace hazards emerged. Here is how some of the industrial temps responded:

-"Yes, there are dangerous conditions. . . . At the Hyatt hotel recently, a renovation project involved moving heavy construction parts with heavy equipment. The whole setup was dangerous."
-"Moving heavy appliances . . . stacking refrigerators, ovens, and microwaves is dangerous work."
-"I had a job installing Sport Courts for a while that was particularly hot work. . . . Heat exhaustion seemed a real possibility."

-"Yes, at the Department of Human Resources . . . I developed back strain from moving oversized filing cabinets all day."

-"The lumberyard was dangerous. . . . Lots of heavy lifting and moving stuff around. New hands make a work site like that more dangerous. A lot of jobs are dangerous in the sense they are heavy jobs and could easily lead to accidents."

-"There are many potential hazards; I've never been hurt, but the possibility is real. . . . You must use great caution."

-"Working with forklifts on the second and third levels of warehouses can pose certain hazards, such as falling off and getting crushed by packaged appliances."

Several temporary industrial workers described their working conditions as uncomfortable rather than dangerous. For example, one complained of "suffering scratches from moving stock around," whereas another worker, who had an assignment installing insulation, lamented the minor but irritating hand, neck, and face lacerations he received. Managers also noted the frequency with which disagreeable conditions were confronted by their workers. One manager, who confirmed that the work could often be strenuous, said there was a strong tendency among employers to think, "Oh well, these are just temps; we can give them all of the shit work." An illustration of this attitude was an employer who directed his temporary industrial worker to hand-sweep a parking lot the size of three football fields in addition to completing similar duties inside. The temporary help manager told the employer to hire additional workers for the job, or she would withdraw the overburdened worker. That this branch manager was ill-informed about workers' actual conditions is apparently not atypical. As Nelson and Mayall noted:

Some recent cases of industrial accidents in large manufacturing plants (specifically chemical producers) which involved Temporary Help Services and other contract workers, suggests that it is very difficult for a THS or other contractor to be fully cognizant of all the safety factors involved . . . and hence to take the necessary steps to insure worker safety.[3]

Among the managers interviewed, only one admitted assigning workers to jobs he knew were dangerous or unhealthy. As an example, this manager cited the willingness of his firm to assign industrial workers to work in chemical companies. Although his firm technically supplied only light industrial workers, he conceded that such working environments posed potential hazards for workers' health. This manager expressed his firm's philosophy this way: "If a worker is aware of the risks, then there is not a problem." To elaborate, he recounted a case of a worker who developed a rash after completing an assignment for a chemical company. "This worker," the manager continued, "should have worn protective clothing. . . . He should have known about the impact without clothing. It's just tough shit for him." Moreover, this manager claimed the major reason chemical companies used temporary workers was to avoid the prospect of legal action brought by adversely affected workers. "Quite simply," he said, "they [chemical company employers] want the temporary services to bear the responsibility for any health problems."

This manager was more candid than others on the subject of temporary workers and health and safety. With little exception, the other managers argued that the occupations considered dangerous or unhealthy were unprofitable because the workers' compensation premiums associated with them were inflated. Among the managers whose firms provided industrial workers, the light part of the industrial category was heavily emphasized. For example, one manager showed me a brochure titled "Employees' Prohibited Occupation List," which identified job assignments the firm was forbidden from filling. Included in the "general" category was "any work of over one story in height indoors or outside, where the use of ladders or scaffolding is required" and work "involving building demolition or other wrecking/dismantling operations." Other "specific" activities forbidden by this temporary company included "work involving logging, lumbering, or saw mill operations, work requiring mixing, handling or using pesticides or poisons, and work where there is exposure to known chemicals."

According to this temporary company's manager, when the company received a request that was forbidden by its policies, it recommended that the employer try the labor pool, the labor corners, or the state's employment commission. Other managers presented a similar outlook on the issue of health and safety. Most characterized it as unprofitable, although one manager did intimate that creative bookkeeping could alleviate some of the "problems" with workers' compensation premiums.

Although work assignments were advertised as light industrial, there was nothing light about the tasks I completed as an employee of the temporary help industry. In terms of physical exertion, I found the assignments comparable to jobs I had held as a construction laborer. When questioned about the light industrial label, temporary managers generally acknowledged it was something of a misnomer, but each stood by its technical correctness.

Conclusion

Temporary industrial workers are similar to temporary clerical workers in that they face the same uncertainty, the same stigma, and the same kind of indifferent treatment from other workers. And perhaps to a greater extent than clerical workers, temporary industrial employees face workplace conditions that pose health and safety hazards. Clerical workers must contend with contaminated indoor air, eyestrain, and headaches and dizziness from using video display terminals, whereas industrial workers confront a different set of potentially dangerous conditions. Despite the routine exposure of temporary workers to health and safety risks, neither clerical nor industrial employees generally have access to health insurance. Whereas all the industrial work assigned is classified as light industrial, in reality it often involves hot and physically demanding, if not hazardous, labor. Finally, the reported use by chemical companies of temporary workers to avoid liability suggests an important function of temporary work for employers.

6

THE GROWTH OF CONTINGENT WORK: A CRITICAL VIEW

ALTHOUGH POPULAR ACCOUNTS and the temporary help industry stress supply-side reasons for the industry's growth, more fundamental political and economic factors appear to carry greater explanatory power. Of particular significance are developments in corporate restructuring (and capital flight), which the public considers legitimate because the United States needs to regain economic competitiveness. This restructuring is truly profound. Massive layoffs in America have led to the creation of a large pool of workers (most of them women) available for contingent employment. Except among day laborers and labor pool workers, women overwhelmingly numerically dominate the various other branches—from the self-employed to moonlighters.

Additional insight into the growth of temporary work can be gleaned from the ideas of Harry Braverman and others in the labor process tradition. This critical school of thought tends to focus our attention on the latent functions that temporary work serves for employers. For instance, deskilling has played an important role in disassembling jobs to make them cheaper.

Corporate Restructuring

Temporary help corporations, their trade associations, and many employers typically emphasize the allegedly mutually beneficial arrangement that temp work presents for both workers and employers. My research suggests little support for this proposition. The notion that recent growth has been due to voluntary participation, mainly by women who want a career and a domestic life, is seriously flawed. It ignores the source of this pool of workers. Many are victims of the wide-scale corporate restructuring (or downsizing) that has been occurring since the early 1970s. The decline of core workers employed by major corporations has been greater in recent years than in any other post–World War II period.[1] In 1970 approximately 19 percent of U.S. workers were employed by Fortune 500 corporations, but by the late 1980s only 12.2 percent were working for these large companies. Despite the headlines about economic recovery, rising worker productivity, and declining joblessness, in the early 1990s major corporations were restructuring and laying off workers in record numbers. Some companies, such as IBM, were laying workers off for the first time in their history. Furthermore, a considerable amount of employment loss was being disguised by the proliferation of contingent arrangements. There is no reliably accurate way to quantify the number of formerly permanent workers who are now accepting part-time and temporary work.

One of the reasons American corporations have been adopting wide-scale layoffs while incorporating flexible working schedules is the genuine economic pressure generated by increasing international competition. But domestic economic competition, in particular the privatization and de-regulatory movements of the 1980s, has also increased. This provides added impetus for employers to reduce their permanent workforces. The deregulatory and privatization movements that led to increased contingent employment were powerfully shaped by the conservative political regimes of the 1970s and 1980s. Under Ronald Reagan and George Bush, the nation's policies toward workers regressed. The decertification of the Professional Air Traffic Controllers Organization after an unsuccessful strike set the stage for how the federal government related to labor and employment issues in the following years.

The financial deregulation of the U.S. economy in the early 1980s heightened corporate America's obsession with short-term, narrowly focused, economic performance. Short-term financing became increasingly commonplace, and along with it came unrelenting pressure on companies burdened with short-term obligations to repay their debt. Perhaps more important, the deregulatory movement led to scores of leveraged buyouts, mergers, hostile takeovers, and corporate raids, which contributed to extensive layoffs. Because of these financially related developments, many large businesses became organizationally less flexible in the 1980s. In turn, this created additional pressure on corporate executives to find other areas of flexibility through layoffs and alterations in work patterns and schedules. The corporate raiding mentality that characterized much of the 1980s caused many otherwise economically healthy companies to take belt-tightening measures to ward off potential raiders.

The Corporate Search for Flexibility

The major impetus in the expansion of temporary work, then, is the growing corporate demand for a flexible workforce. Employers are pursuing several types of flexibility in their efforts to remain competitive and increase profitability. After reviewing research undertaken at the Institute of Manpower at Sussex, *The Economist* concluded that companies are seeking a mix of three kinds of flexibility: functional flexibility (to allow workers to transfer their repetitive task performance to other jobs requiring repetition), numerical flexibility (to enable employers to fluctuate workers in tune with the vagaries of the business cycle), and financial flexibility (to permit rapid layoffs without incurring extra costs).[2]

The newsweekly noted that in the flexible company there are several distinct internal labor markets. For example, in the "core," upwardly mobile managers and technicians provide functional flexibility, allowing themselves to be transferred from one job to another within a division or plant. Skills in the core are particularistic, acquired over time, and not easily purchased from the external labor market. In the "first periphery," there are full-time jobs but no progressive career trajectories. Positions such as clerks, assemblers, and supervisors may provide some job security but are dead-end; thus turnover tends to be high. This high turnover provides the organization with an important degree of numerical flexibility. In the "second periphery," there are part-time workers, job-sharing arrangements, two-tier wage workers, and other types of employees working on short-term contracts. All these categories provide the company with numerical flexibility. Finally, there are the "externals"—workers from temporary help services, business service (subcontracting) firms, and others employed on a contingent or temporary basis. The externals provide the company with a final measure of functional, numerical, and financial flexibility.

Anna Pollert described a model in which a firm's workers offer two types of flexibility. The first is functional flexibility, secured by having a pool of workers easily able to cross occupational boundaries. The second is numerical flexibility, obtained by having workers who are "insecurely or irregularly employed." Both types are used to enhance a firm's flexibility in terms of "its adaptability to expansion, contraction or change in the product market."[3]

Even though temporary workers provide employers with substantial flexibility in their organizational structure, corporations continue to experiment with cost-saving initiatives such as offshore employment, prison labor, and wholesale capital flight. Clearly, these strategies are centered on minimizing costs and increasing profits by heightening labor exploitation.

Attacking the Social Wage to Achieve Flexibility

Barry Bluestone and Bennett Harrison contributed to the view that the expansion of temporary work can largely be explained in terms of the corporate demand for flexible workers.[4] In *The Deindustrialization of America*, the authors highlighted the corporate response to the stagflation of the late 1960s and 1970s. They discussed the efforts of corporate managers to find new, more profitable uses for their capital and new ways of cutting production costs in their operations. Bluestone and Harrison identified "buying and selling entire businesses and transferring capital from one sector to another" as the most important corporate strategies for raising and protecting short-term profitability (p. 164). Furthermore, they noted the role of "differentially expand[ing] and contract[ing]" facilities as an important strategy, one that involved circumventing unions and the active pursuit of "good business climates" (pp. 164, 180). As their work documented, many corporations left the north for the south and then left the country altogether. In addition, the conservative political climate that pervaded the 1980s helped foster a cottage industry of sophisticated consulting firms to implement expensive antiunion campaigns.

The connection between Bluestone and Harrison's analysis and temporary work emerges most clearly in their consideration of capital's assault on the social wage. They observed that "because so few American workers belong to unions, these managerial responses were not sufficient to make really significant, long-term dents in labor costs" (p. 180). To achieve greater cost cutting, employers set upon a calculated campaign to make all workers more flexible. Public and private employers alike, along with their political allies, attempted to make nonworking alternatives to contingent jobs unbearable, to make workers desperate and anxious enough to take any job, regardless of pay or workplace conditions. Important elements in this campaign in the 1980s were sustained attacks on the minimum wage, Social Security, public health programs, and unemployment insurance. Faced with a reduced safety net, part-time and temporary jobs became more appealing "choices" for workers.

Bluestone and Harrison's stress on the organizational drive to reduce labor costs coincides with the expanding use of temporary workers by corporations undergoing restructuring. In particular, two important functions of temporary employment help meet employers' efforts to cut labor costs deeply. In the language of the temporary help industry, the first is simply known as a "cost-control" function. Companies that employ temporary workers can strictly control labor costs by avoiding fringe benefit and related personnel expenditures.

The second strategy is known as planned staffing and enables employers to reduce labor costs further through a more systematic use of temporary workers. With this approach additional savings accrue as employers can maintain a minimum number of permanent workers on their payrolls. Any fluctuations in demand for the com-

panies' products or services can be absorbed by temporary employees, the use of whom eliminates any potential morale problem
among the permanently employed or burdensome unemployment
insurance premiums.

The use of sizable numbers of temporary workers in a deliberate,
long-term approach within firms developed largely as a result of the
economic contractions of the 1970s and the 1980s. The rapidity with
which each new recession arrived, along with the recessions' growing severity, caused employers to become more sensitive to all types
of costs, especially labor-related ones. As many corporate executives
see the situation, the fastest way to reduce costs is to dismiss workers.
Given the U.S. economy's recessionary history, employers have remained reluctant to hire permanent workers (despite the economic
expansion of the 1980s) and have intensified the use of mass layoffs
and contingent working arrangements. As Daniel Struve noted:

> There's little doubt that the end of the [1980–1982] recession had a great
> impact on the temporary employment field. Companies forced to lay off
> employees earlier in the decade are now experiencing a renewed need for
> them. But many firms are gun-shy. They don't want to hire a new staff and
> then be forced to lay them off if a similar economic downturn occurs.[5]

Prior to the temporary help industry's innovative marketing of the
planned staffing approach, employers hired additional temporary
workers during peakload periods, such as when retail stores add
sales staff during the Christmas season or when the IRS expands
employment each spring. These former methods, although thoroughly rationalized in themselves, fall short of the comprehensive
planned staffing strategy. Employers have made a relatively quick
transition from using temporary workers during peakload periods
to using them as a buffer against the cyclical gyrations characteristic
of the planned staffing approach. Planned staffing involves the full-
time, year-round use of temporary workers to serve as a continual
buffer against downturns in the business cycle, fluctuations in demand resulting from seasonal differences, or any other major
variations.

Employers' adoption of the planned staffing strategy is part and
parcel of the drive among American corporations to implement a
"lean and mean" organizational structure. As NATS spokesperson

Sam Sacco observed, "With the recovery continually in rebound, the expected leveling off of temporary workers has not happened. It may be that employers have seen the wisdom of keeping their permanent staffs trim and hiring temps as needed."[6]

Not all agree that corporate America has seen the advantage in maintaining an extensive corps of temporary workers. Some industry executives express skepticism about the lean and mean thesis. Notably, Mitchell Fromstein said, "It's an old bromide. . . . You hear that in this industry after every downturn, when the pain of recession is fresh in the minds of management."[7] But Fromstein's assertion is a dissenting position. The consensus view among industry leaders and local managers is that the planned staffing personnel approach has been embraced enthusiastically by employers. One manager told me, "The temporary help industry is pushing planned staffing. It is only five years old and has rapidly become a key selling point for the services. At least 60 percent of all the firms using temporary workers are doing so for planned staffing reasons."

Within this shared view, however, considerable disagreement exists among industry leaders concerning how far planned staffing can and does extend. The manager just quoted took the position that "with planned staffing, you can keep the very minimum number of permanent workers on the payroll." Others thought planned staffing worked best when utilized sparingly. Some described the expansion of temporary workers in different terms. For example, a senior vice-president at Kelly Services carefully couched the issue by arguing that "managers are looking to employ a baseline level of staff, the people they need to get out the business they've got. The overstaffing of the past has largely been set aside, for good, sound personnel reasons."[8] Similarly, the president of Uniforce Temporary Services said that behind much of the boom in the industry "is a burgeoning commitment by business to lean, year-round, permanent staffing that can be supplemented with temporaries as workloads expand. Companies are increasingly reluctant to add to fixed expenses."[9]

Several managers of temporary help firms identified the same local employer to illustrate the use of the planned staffing strategy. According to these managers, during the 1981–1982 recession Motorola laid off three hundred temporary workers while avoiding any cuts in permanent staff and thereby convinced many employers of the advantages of planned staffing. In the vernacular of employers and the temporary help industry, several benefits accrued from this "head count adjustment."

According to the managers, a prominent advantage of using contingent workers is that employers can use them to construct an acceptable public image. In the Motorola case, a major U.S. employer was able to unobtrusively release its "excess" workers while news accounts about layoffs at other high-technology companies appeared daily in the local news media. In addition to upholding the company's reputation in the community, Motorola was able to sustain morale among full-time workers by preserving their jobs. This action meant also that any unemployment insurance claims filed by ex-workers were not the responsibility of the electronics firm but of the temporary firms that employed them. For all these reasons, Motorola, along with many other high-tech firms, has continued to refine the practice of employing temporary workers as a buffer against economic downswings.

Even Mitchell Fromstein, who had earlier called the lean and mean thesis an "old bromide," altered his posture. He saw a much more extensive acceptance of the planned staffing strategy. In explaining the intensified use of temporary employees, Fromstein stated:

> The unusual element of this recovery is the hesitation of companies to overstaff, which used to happen. They're now concerned with maintaining a core workforce. . . . Hiring people when business is good and then firing them as business sours is expensive. What is more, it's disrupting to employees. Especially with larger companies, the desire is not to have this roller-coaster syndrome when it comes to the workforce."[10]

In addition to providing immediate financial flexibility for employers, planned staffing gradually but steadily erodes the permanent full-time workforce. Planned staffing is a particularly critical development in human resource management because it encourages a growing and expanding use of temporary workers. The potential savings accruing from planned staffing are far more substantial than any of the other ways temporary workers are employed. Using the planned staffing human resources approach is roughly analogous to having a formally bureaucratized reserve army of the unemployed at an employer's disposal. With temporary workers readily available, the employer has an ample supply of employees to draw upon when business is expanding and the capacity to make quick layoffs when economic conditions tighten. With many temporary workers already seeking full-time employment, the expansion of planned staffing as a routine personnel policy depresses wages and working conditions among all U.S. workers.

It is difficult to predict to what extent planned staffing will ultimately reduce the demand for full-time, permanent workers. But clearly some organizations are willing to transfer a significant part of their permanent workforce to temporary and part-time status. As noted in Chapter 3, employers at community colleges have found it cost-effective to employ as much as half their faculty on a part-time, temporary basis. Other organizations have extended the proportion of their contingent workforce to 70 percent. In short, the systematic planned staffing approach is an important catalyst serving to perpetuate and expand the ranks of temporary workers.

The intensification of temporary worker usage on a permanent basis is just one element of a broader drive by private- and public-sector employers to cut labor costs. As noted earlier, the U.S. core economy increasingly relies on a range of contingent workers, from part-time and low-wage workers to independent contractors and in-house temps. Ruth Walker pointed out that advances in the growing importance of flexible and leaner permanent staffs are "seen as part of a larger trend toward . . . companies' contracting out all sorts of support services from pension fund management to watering the plants around the office."[11] The nearly obsessive concern for flexibility that swept through corporate America in the 1970s and 1980s is central to understanding the expansion of temporary and other forms of contingent labor, such as part-time employment.

Using Part-Time Workers to Promote Flexibility

Employers are also hiring greater numbers of part-time workers on a permanent basis as part of their strategy to maximize worker flexibility. As noted earlier, part-time work grew more rapidly than did the labor force as a whole during the 1970s and 1980s. But perhaps more important than the sheer growth are the roles part-time workers are serving for employers. Part-time workers often provide organizations with many of the same benefits as temporary employees do.

First, employers enjoy the immediate advantage of saving significantly in labor costs. In 1990 part-time workers earned a median hourly wage of $5.06, compared with $8.09 for full-time workers. Second, the expanding use of part-time workers applies downward pressure in outlays for fringe benefit costs; few part-time employees receive paid holidays, sick pay, vacations, health insurance, or pensions. Third, like temporary workers, part-time workers tend to undermine the struggle for job security; both part-time and temporary employees can be summarily dismissed.

Fourth, part-time employees can be used to maximize organizational productivity. For example, employers often specifically hire part-time employees to work during peak periods. Financial institutions are among the pioneers of routinely using part-time employees. A typical example involves the Provident Bank in Cincinnati, which implemented a part-time program among its 270 formerly full-time service tellers in the mid-1980s. Within a year half the tellers were working strictly on a peak-time arrangement. Not only do many financial institutions now employ tellers only part time; they often break up tellers' work schedules to coincide with rush periods. The use of part-time workers on a peakload basis is gaining popularity in other industries as well. These illustrations clearly suggest that employers are actively striving to create a flexible workforce. Organizations are not content to wait for workers to volunteer for contingent positions. Temporary help companies are not complacent either, aggressively marketing their "products" to potential clients.

For employers flexibility is a multifaceted concept. Among firms that embrace a comprehensive flexible human resource model, the result is a finely divided workforce. With the increasing use of temporary and part-time workers, employers are reaping additional privileges by dividing, segmenting, and marginalizing their workforces.

Other Theoretical Views: Latent Functions of Temporary Work

Another, seldom recognized, reason for the progressive advance in temporary work is the variety of latent functions contingent workers serve for employers. Enhancing management control over workers within the workplace is one such understudied function. For instance, by aggressively advertising the advantages of using temporary workers, the temporary help industry has persuaded many employers to incorporate them into multiple phases of company operations. Temporary, part-time, and contingent workers can help facilitate workplace control because they are not perceived or treated as members of the full-time workforce. Instead, contingent workers are regarded by management as merely another resource in the production process.

Management control in the workplace can also become more finely tuned through the use of a "core and contingent" hiring arrangement of the type described previously. As part of creating this type of structure, companies can use temporary help firms as a screening mechanism for potential full-time workers. Although employers are legally sanctioned from recruiting workers through temporary help firms, 12 percent of respondents in one survey said their organizations used temporary employees for possible permanent recruitment.[12] Thus if employers want a docile workforce (or a white or male workforce), they can eventually assemble one through a deliberate, calculated selection of temporary, subcontracted, and part-time workers. This approach to human relations can be doubly rewarding for employers as it spares them labor costs along with the time usually consumed by recruiting and hiring.

Gottfried has shown that temporary help firms have developed new forms of worker control for employers. Her research revealed a dual system of control. First, temporary help firms indirectly control workers. Second, temporary firms "rationalize" jobs within an employer's organization by establishing a set of tasks, competencies, and responsibilities. Gottfried's case study demonstrated the key role temporary firms can play in controlling workers from outside the workplace, a role increasingly necessitated by the flexible firm of the 1990s.[13]

Thwarting Workplace Organization

Another commonly overlooked function that temporary workers serve for employers is inhibiting worker organization efforts. As many managers view it, temporary workers are a new division to exploit within the workplace. As Richard Edwards demonstrated, U.S. capitalism has fractured, rather than unified, the working class.[14] Workers are divided by industrial sector, age, race, sex, and skill level. With the expansion of contingent labor, workers are further subdivided by their schedules and the daily working conditions they confront. Dividing workers provides managers with immediate labor cost savings while helping limit opportunities for worker mobilization and organization. Temporary employees are especially effective in blunting organizing efforts because managers frequently hire them one day dismiss them the next and thus virtually eliminate any opportunity for politically oriented activity to occur at the workplace. Indeed, temporary workers can organize a union only at their place of employment (the temporary firm), not at the workplaces where they are assigned, further reducing the opportunity for solidarity. In addition, temps may be viewed by many permanent workers as a threat to their jobs or their wages. In some cases temporary workers are treated like scabs.[15] Temporary workers seldom are at their true employer's office; most information and work assignments are handled over the phone.

Further impeding organizing efforts are the relative isolation temporary workers face, the fact that contingent workers do not stay with the same employer for extended periods, and the fact that they have more than one employer. Together these factors provide a major tactical advantage for employers. As a case in point, in the early 1980s Blue Shield used temporary workers to avoid negotiating with its workers' union. After a three-month strike by members of the Office and Professional Employees Union Local 3, the insurance giant hired more than 450 temporary workers to staff a claims processing office in a suburban neighborhood. A letter sent to the union simply stated, "The company finds work can be performed for the most part much more competitively in other labor markets where compensation, benefits, and facilities are less expensive."[16] The additional layer of contingent employees in the workplace may also obstruct the ability of full-time workers to maintain solidarity. Joseph McKendrick succinctly expressed the benefit of using temporary workers this way: "A temporary worker comes in fresh, alert and ready to work, and is not socially or politically involved with other workers."[17]

The Intermediary Role

Temporary help firms, business service companies, and employee leasing firms further enhance workplace control by serving as an intermediary between workers and employers of temporary help. Along with freeing employers from what is widely regarded as burdensome paperwork, temporary help firms enable employers to avoid the disagreeable task of terminating workers. Moreover, the temporary help industry benefits employers because it is often able to perform personnel functions more expediently than can the practices dictated by many major corporations. In most cases, for example, an employer of temporary workers can have a worker removed any time during the first working day free of charge if the employer is not satisfied with that worker's performance.

Other Latent Functions

Temporary workers serve still other subtle and often hidden functions for employers. By filling high-turnover positions with temporary employees, for example, employers can divert frustration over working conditions among permanent workers. In particular, tiring or boring jobs or ones that feature irregular hours are typical positions that employers increasingly staff with contingent workers to avoid high turnover rates among the permanent workforce. Interviews with managers of temporary firms confirmed that their employees were sometimes hired for permanent part-time positions this way, especially in the case of unskilled clerks and unskilled manual laborers. One manager said that in high turnover situations, she encouraged employers to place the temporary worker in the boring slot to free up more challenging positions for permanent employees. Robert Gibson, CEO of Norrell Services, lent support to this position by claiming that "temporary workers can function with real commitment since they are free from fear of dead-end stagnation. The repetitious nature of the work need not be viewed as endless."[18] And Sacco explained that "sometimes an employer will have a job with high turnover—it's just too boring for anyone to do it for long— so he'll hire a temporary worker who knows he doesn't have to do it forever."[19]

In addition to filling jobs that are monotonous, tiring, or otherwise undesirable, temporary workers are called upon to do a disproportionate share of dangerous jobs. As noted earlier, one manager cited the use of temporary workers in chemical companies as one area where temporary employees routinely face occupational hazards. A more dramatic example is the transformation of temporary workers into disposable commodities in the nuclear utility industry.

Deskilling and Temporary Work

Harry Braverman's *Labor and Monopoly Capital* (1974) offers a critical perspective on the labor process that sheds additional light on the emergence and expansion of temporary work. The book provides an intriguing critique of the capitalist labor process as it evolved during the course of the twentieth century.[20] Braverman's central thesis is that given capitalistic control of the workplace, there has been, and continues to be, a long-term tendency toward the mechanization, fragmentation, and rationalization of work. The result is an increasingly deskilled workforce, one that steadily witnesses the transference of traditional craft skills and scientific knowledge to new managerial positions and modern production technologies. Since publication, Braverman's ideas have stimulated considerable scholarly discourse and debate.

Braverman's conceptual framework can be applied to the developments discussed in the preceding chapters. Over time the gradual deskilling process has acted as a fundamental social force that has permitted (indeed, driven) temporary, part-time, and other forms of contingent work to flourish. As we have seen, at the center of employers' personnel efforts today is the creation of a highly flexible, interchangeable workforce. Contingent workers generally, and temporary workers particularly, epitomize the interchangeability that deskilling fosters. Through the interconnected processes of specialization and standardization, deskilling has laid the foundation for temporary employment.

Temporary help firms are profitable because they capitalize on the existence of enormous numbers of unskilled and semiskilled jobs that have high absenteeism and turnover rates. Meanwhile the industry's profitability is stabilized by employers that recognize that the average worker can fill in quickly and effectively at many diverse occupations with little training. Indeed, as the temporary help industry likes to claim, some temporary workers may be more skilled (because of their resourcefulness and adaptability) than the permanently employed. But the fundamental point remains that both groups have become sufficiently deskilled that they can be interchanged with minimal workplace disruption.

Deskilling is pivotal not only in helping create the preconditions for contingent employment but also in serving as a catalyst once the foundation for flexible working arrangements has been laid. Despite conventional wisdom concerning the need for upgrading the skills of clerical skill workers, many of the workers that use new automated office systems are progressively becoming deskilled. Much of the new automated equipment significantly reduces skill requirements and the need for decision making. Automated systems also present managers with new sophisticated techniques for monitoring and controlling workers.

In the contemporary bureaucratic, technologically advanced office, many traditional secretarial skills have been diminished. The proletarianization of the clerical workforce documented by C. Wright Mills and Harry Braverman continues to evolve and is now entering a heightened phase. With the introduction of automated office systems, there is less and less need for clerical workers to exert discretion in the workplace. In this way the deskilling of clerical work facilitates the expansion of contingent employment. Through temporary help companies, subcontractors, and business services, employers are reaping the benefits of the decades-long deskilling process. Contingent workers are not effective in replacing workers with firm-specific skills. Rather, temporary employees are cost-effective when they can be quickly and easily interchanged.

The interchangeability fostered by deskilling is intensified by the trend toward the use of electronic data processing systems. Deskilling provides a foundation for contingent work and, through a progressive erosion of traditional occupational skills, steadily produces new opportunities for growth in the temporary help industry. The impact of deskilling manifested in automation is transforming the character of clerical positions. And in the process, it is making more clerical occupations conducive to part-time and temporary restructuring.

Conclusion

Temporary employment has expanded as employers have sought to create a flexible workforce. Affected by the experience of recent recessions, along with increasing domestic and international competition, many corporate executives have aimed to minimize the year-round, full-time segment of their workforce. Temporary workers are just one consequence of this pursuit of flexibility. Casual workers, part-time workers, the resurrection of sweatshops, at-home work, the advent of the offshore office, and other varieties of contingent employment have all surfaced from similar pressures.

The progressive deskilling of occupations has enabled the temporary help industry to become prominent and highly profitable in the 1990s. The industry's current success exploits many millions of workers employed at unskilled and semiskilled jobs. Then as the deskilling process continues to unfold, eroding workers' traditional training and skills, more occupations become accessible to servicing by the temporary help industry.

There are also key latent benefits that temporary workers offer to employers, including enhancing management control of the workplace. An important aspect of this greater control is the use of temporary workers to undermine organizing efforts within the workplace. The creation of a readily available contingent workforce has divided workers. The companies that constitute the temporary help industry have erected obstacles to communication and mobilization among workers. The managerial drive for flexible organizations has resulted in temps pitting themselves against permanent workers. Temporary employees, who are "willing" to work in unpredictable and ever-changing circumstances and for one-third less compensation, under-mine the pay and working conditions of full-time workers. Taken together, the political and economic benefits to employers from using temporary workers are significant. Temporary workers can be a highly sophisticated instrument for employers, part of an overall staffing strategy that facilitates management's control over the labor process and maximizes the potential output of every hour of paid labor.

APPENDIX

Interview Schedules

I asked the following questions of the eleven managers of temporary help firms.

1. Location:
   Firm:
   Date and time:
   Respondent:
2. How many clerical and industrial temporary workers does your company employ during a given month?
3. How large is the pool of workers you have to work with to fill temporary assignments?
4. How many applicants do you see during a given week?
5. What percentage of your assignments are for clerical workers as opposed to those for industrial workers?
6. What kinds of work do your clerical workers perform? Your industrial workers?
7. What are the major occupational titles your workers are assigned?
8. What occupations do employers avoid filling with temporary workers?
9. How long does the typical temporary assignment last? What percentage last longer than three days? One week? One month?
10. How long does the average worker stay with your company? How many stay as long as one month? Three months? One year?
11. What industries use your workers most heavily?

12. Who are some of the biggest users of temporary help in this area? Please briefly describe the type of contract you have with them.
13. What kind of person do you think performs well as a temporary worker? Are there any special traits or characteristics that make a temporary worker effective?
14. What kind of person typically does not perform satisfactorily as a temporary?
15. What minimum qualifications must a worker possess to be employed as a temporary? Does he or she have to own a phone and car? What about minimum formal education?
16. Do you provide training of any kind?
17. Please characterize the typical applicant for temporary work.
    -"Housewives looking for pin money"?
    -"Transients, drifters"?
    -"New to town"?
    -"Those supplementing income while looking for full-time work"?
    -"'Laid-back' types seeking greater leisure time"?
18. What is the demographic composition of your temporary workforce?
    -% white   -% black   -% hispanic   -% other
    -Marital status   -Age (typical and range)   -Sex
19. Presently, clerical and industrial workers are the mainstays of the temporary help industry. Do you see the use of temporary work making any significant inroads into other occupational fields? Which ones? Why?
20. What are some of the major reasons that companies use temporary workers? What would you say is the greatest single reason?
    -To replace sick or vacationing workers?
    -To use as a "screening mechanism" or recruitment tool?
    -To function as a part of "planned staffing"?
    -To cut costs?
    -Other?
21. What new trends do you see in the use of temporary workers? What are some newly emerging reasons employers are using temporary workers?
22. How do you market your services?

23. Do you spend more time recruiting clients or temporary workers?
24. What kinds of arguments do you use to try convincing employers to use temporary workers? What are your key selling points?
25. Have you had much trouble recruiting clerical or industrial temporary workers?
26. How much orientation time do your clerical workers require before they can be productively at work?
27. How often have you sent workers on an assignment that you thought might be dangerous or unhealthy?
28. How much variety in assignments is there for clerical and industrial temporary workers?
29. Do you have any way of knowing what happens to the people who formerly filled temporary assignments for your firm? If so, please elaborate.
30. What proportion of your temporary workforce is looking for full-time jobs?
31. How many in your pool would you say are using temporary work as a way to shop for full-time employment?
32. What are some advantages you would identify that employees enjoy when working on a temporary basis?
33. What are some of the disadvantages?
34. What would you say accounts for the rapid growth the temporary help industry has experienced in recent years?
35. Do you see any issues on the horizon that may limit the industry's growth rate?
36. Do you see any other kind of economic or organizational factors that will affect this industry?
37. How does the pay of your clerical and industrial temporary workers differ from the pay of those they are assigned to work with?
38. How do benefits vary?
39. What percentage of your temps would you say eventually go to work full time for a firm they originally temped for?
40. Is there any occupational mobility to speak of in the temporary help industry? Can workers move up in any way? Are there any plum jobs, positions, or employers?

41. How do you recruit temporary workers? How do you retain them? Is any specific mechanism designed to foster commitment?

42. Demographics:
    -Position?
    -Education?
    -Tenure with this company?
    -How long has the company been operating in this city?

43. What can you tell me about your company in terms of its history, organizational structure, and management philosophy?

44. What differences, if any, do you see among temporary help firms?

45. How do you spend your typical day?

46. Do you have any suggestions for finding out more about temporary employment?

The following are the open-ended guiding questions I administered to each of the forty-two workers who completed the entire survey instrument. For a host of reasons other workers could answer only part of the survey. For this reason their responses were not used in shaping the picture of temporary worklife that emerges in this book.

1. How long have you worked as a temporary employee?

2. How long have you worked with this particular temporary firm?

3. What types of work have you been doing as a temporary worker?

4. What kinds of skills and training are required for you to work as a temporary employee?

5. What kinds of new skills have you learned since becoming a temporary worker?

6. Please describe the kinds of permanent work experience you have had.

7. How long does the typical temporary assignment last?

8. What have been your shortest- and longest-lasting assignments?

9. What kind of person do you think performs well as a temporary? What personal attributes are important?

10. How much do you usually earn per hour working as a temporary employee?

11. What were the highest and the lowest amounts you earned working as a temporary employee?

12. What do you like best about being employed as a temporary worker?

13. What do you like least about working as a temporary?

14. What kinds of factors affect the degree of job satisfaction or dissatisfaction you experience? Briefly discuss how each of the following affects your job satisfaction as a temporary worker:
    -Management style
    -Pay and benefits
    -Ability to have some "say" in how work is done
    -Physical work environment
    -Job security/steady earnings

15. Have you experienced any occupational mobility since working as a temporary (in other words, have you moved up or down in terms of prestige, pay, responsibility, etc. since starting to work as a temporary employee)?

16. Would you recommend working as a temporary to a friend, child, or relative?-Why or why not?

17. Would you prefer to be working on a full-time, year-round basis? Why or why not?

18. Are you currently seeking full-time employment? Why or why not?

19. How long do you expect to be working as a temporary employee? Please elaborate.

20. What kinds of fringe benefits have you received since working as a temporary? Have you received vacation pay, holiday pay, health insurance, child care, or bonuses?

21. How many temporary firms are you signed up to work for? Please identify.

22. What kinds of differences do you see among different temporary help firms (if applicable)?

23. Why did you first begin working temporary assignments?

24. How much time elapsed between the time you applied for work and your first assignment?

25. What have been the shortest and the longest periods between assignments?
26. To what extent have you been getting as much work as you want working as a temporary? Please elaborate.
27. How many hours have you typically worked per week as a temporary employee?
28. Have you ever been sent on an assignment that you considered dangerous or unhealthy? If yes, please explain any specific potential hazards.
29. Have you ever been sent on an assignment for which you were overqualified? How often do you feel underutilized when working temporary assignments? How often do you feel underqualified to handle the responsibilities required to complete an assignment?
30. Demographics
    -Name
    -Age
    -Sex
    -Race/ethnicity
    -Last year of formal education

NOTES

1. Contingent Work and the New Economy

1. Richard Belous. *The Contingent Economy: The Growth of the Temporary, Part-Time and Subcontracted Workforce* (Washington, D.C.: National Planning Association, 1989).

2. See John F. Stinson, Jr., "Multiple Jobholding up Sharply in the 1980's," *Monthly Labor Review* 113 (July 1990):3–10; Chris Tilly, "Reasons for the Continuing Growth of Part-Time Employment," *Monthly Labor Review* 114 (March 1991):10–18; Joanne Scherer, "Leasing Employees Catching on," *Las Vegas Review-Journal*, February 5, 1990; Albert B. Crenshaw, "Firms Turning to 'Rent-a-Staff'," *Washington Post*, January 14, 1990, sec. H.; and Rosalind Resnick, "Leasing Workers," *Nation's Business* 80 (11) (1992):20–28.

3. Virginia L. duRivage, "New Policies for the Part-Time and Contingent Workforce," *Briefing Paper* (Washington, D.C.: Economic Policy Institute, November 1991).

4. See Susan McHenry and Linda Lee Small, "Does Part-Time Pay Off?" *Ms.* 3 (1989):88–94; and Kathleen Christensen, "Women and Contingent Work," *Social Policy* 17 (Spring 1987):15–18.

5. Belous, *The Contingent Economy*, p. viii.

6. Jeffrey Pfeffer and James N. Baron, "Taking the Workers Back Out: Recent Trends in the Structuring of Employment," *Research in Organizational Behavior* 10 (1988):257–303.

7. See Anne E. Polivka and Thomas Nardone, "On the Definition of Contingent work," *Monthly Labor Review* 112 (December 1989):9–17.

8. See "Rising Use of Part-Time and Temporary Workers: Who Benefits and Who Loses?" *Hearing Before a Subcommittee of the Committee on Government Operations* (Washington, D.C.: GPO, 1988).

9. Charles Grigsby, "Work," In Donald J. Bauman, Cheryl Beauvais, Charles Grigsby, and D. Franklin Schultz, "The Austin Homeless" (Austin: University of Texas, 1985 Mimeographed), pp. 117–144.

10. Hector Tobar, "L.A. Opens Day-Laborer Hiring Site to All Comers," *Los Angeles Times*, October 27, 1989, sec. A.

11. Colleen Barry, "Hiring Halls Being Revived," *Las Vegas Review-Journal*, November 23, 1990, sec. C.

12. Howard Kimeldorf, *Reds or Rackets?: The Making of Radical and Conservative Unions on the Waterfront* (Berkeley and Los Angeles: University of California Press, 1988).

13. Gil Klein, "In Florida Cane Fields, Immigration Reform Bill Is Hot Topic," *Christian Science Monitor*, September 2, 1983.

14. U.S. House of Representatives, Committee on Education and Labor, Subcommittee on Labor Standards, "Job Rights of Domestic Workers: The Florida Sugar Cane Industry" (Washington, D.C.: GPO, 19983); and Klein, "In Florida Cane Fields, Immigration Reform Bill Is Hot Topic."

15. Belous, *The Contingent Economy*, pp. 22-23.

16. Randy Hodson and Teresa A. Sullivan, *The Social Organization of Work* (Belmont, Calif.: Wadsworth, 1990), p. 308; *Statistical Abstract of the United States, 1993* (Washington, D.C.: GPO, 1993), p. 406.

17. Louis Silverman and Susan J. Dennis, "The Temporary Help Industry: Annual Update," pp. 1-4, reprint from *Contemporary Times* (Spring 1990).

18. See Hodson and Sullivan *The Social Organization of Work*, p. 311.

19. National Association of Temporary Services, "Profile of a Typical Temporary Employee," pp. 1-2, reprint from *Contemporary Times* (Winter 1989).

20. See Diane E. Herz, "Worker Displacement in a Period of Rapid Job Expansion: 1983-87," *Monthly Labor Review* 113 (May 1990):21-33; and Diane E. Herz, "Worker Displacement Still Common in the Late 1980s," *Monthly Labor Review* 114 (May 1991):3-9.

21. Steven A. Wasser, "Economics of the Temporary Help Services Industry," *Contemporary Times* 3(9) (1984):14.

22. Dennis and Silverman, "The Temporary Help Industry."

23. See U.S. Department of Labor, Women's Bureau, *Flexible Workstyles: A Look at Contingent Labor* (Washington, D.C.: GPO.

24. McHenry and Small, "Does Part-Time Pay Off?" p. 88.

25. Tilly, Chris, "Reasons for the Continuing Growth of Part-time Employment," *Monthly Labor Review* 114 (March 1991):10.

26. William Serrin, "Up to a Fifth of U.S. Workers Now Rely on Part-Time Jobs." *New York Times*, August 14, 1983, sec A.

27. Data cited in Polly Callaghan and Heidi Hartmann, *Contingent Work: A Chartbook on Part-Time and Temporary Employment* (Washington, D.C.: Economic Policy Institute, 1991), p. 4.

28. Peter Kilborn, "Part-Time Hirings Bring Deep Change in U.S. Workplaces," *New York Times*, June 17, 1991, sec. A.

29. See Sharon Canter, "The Temporary Help Industry: Filling the Needs of Workers and Business," in U.S. Department of Labor, *Flexible Workstyles*, pp. 46-49.

30. Mack Moore, *"The Role of Temporary Help Services in the Clerical Labor Market"* (Ph.D. diss., University of Wisconsin, 1963). See also Mack Moore, "The Temporary Help Service Industry: Historical Development, Operation and Scope," *Industrial and Labor Relations Review* 18(4) (1965):549-569; Garth Mangum, Donald Mayall, and Kristin Nelson, "The Temporary Help Industry: A Response to the Dual Internal Labor Market," *Industrial and Labor Relations Review* 38(4) (1985):599-611; Martin J. Gannon, "An Analysis of the Temporary Help Industry," in *Labor Market Intermediaries*, Special Report no. 22 of the National Commission for Manpower Policy (Wash-

ington, D.C.: GPO, 1978), pp. 195–225; Martin J. Gannon, "Preferences of Temporary Workers: Time, Variety, and Flexibility," *Monthly Labor Review* 107 (August 1984):26–27; Mitchell Fromstein, *The Socio-Economic Roles of the Temporary Help Service in the United States Labor Market* (Washington, D.C.: National Commission for Manpower Policy, 1977); Richard Leone and Donald Burke, *Women Returning to Work and Their Interaction with a Temporary Help Service* (Springfield, Va.: National Technical Information Service, 1976); and Donald Mayall and Kristin Nelson, *The Temporary Help Supply Service and the Temporary Labor Market* (Salt Lake City: Olympus Research, 1982).

31. Mangum et al., "The Temporary Help Industry," p. 609.

32. See Veronica Beechey and Tessa Perkins, *A Matter of Hours: Women, Part-Time Work and the Labour Market* (Minneapolis: University of Minnesota Press, 1987). See also Eileen Applebaum, "Restructuring Work: Temporary, Part-Time, and At-Home Employment," in Heidi Hartmann, Robert E. Kraut, and Louise A. Tilly (eds.), *Computer Chips and Paper Clips: Technology and Women's Employment* (Washington, D.C.: National Academy Press, 1987) pp. 268–310; Callaghan and Hartmann, *Contingent Work;* 9 to 5, National Association of Working Women, *Working at the Margins: Part-Time and Temporary Workers in the United States* (Cleveland: National Association of Working Women, 1986); June Lapidus, *The Temporary Help Industry and the Operation of the Labor Market* Ph.D. diss., University of Massachusetts, 1990).

33. Cited in Callaghan and Hartmann, *Contingent Work,* p. 7.

34. Ibid., p. 6.

35. See Sar A. Levitan and Elizabeth A. Conway, "Part-timers: Living on Half-Rations," *Challenge* 31 (5–6) (1988):9–16; and U.S. Department of Labor, *A Profile of the Working Poor,* Bureau of Labor Statistics Bulletin 2345 (Washington, D.C.: GPO, December 1989).

36. Sar A. Levitan and Isaac Shapiro, *Working But Poor* (Baltimore: Johns Hopkins University Press, 1987); and U.S. Department of Labor, *Linking Employment Problems to Economic Status,* Bureau of Labor Statistics Bulletin 2282 (Washington, D.C.: GPO, 1987).

37. Deborah Wise, Aaron Bernstein, and Alice Z. Cuneo, "Part-Time Workers: Rising Numbers, Rising Discord," U.S. Department of Labor, *Linking Employment Problems to Economic Status,* Bureau of Labor Statistics Bulletin 2282 (Washington, D.C.: GPO, 1987). *Business Week,* April 1, 1985, pp. 62–63.

38. U.S. Department of Labor, *Linking Employment Problems to Economic Status;* and U.S. Department of Labor, *A Profile of the Working Poor.*

39. U.S. Department of Labor, *Linking Employment Problems to Economic Status.*

40. Daniel H. Saks, *Distressed Workers in the 80's* (Washington, D.C.: National Planning Association 1983). See also Teresa A. Sullivan, *Marginal Workers, Marginal Jobs* (Austin: University of Texas Press, 1978); and U.S. Department of Labor, *Linking Employment Problems to Economic Status.*

41. 9 to 5, *Working at the Margins.* See also duRivage, "New Policies for the Part-Time and Contingent Workforce"; Southern Regional Council, *Hard Labor: A Report on Day Labor Pools and Temporary Employment* (Atlanta: Southern Regional Council, 1988).

42. Sar A. Levitan and Robert Taggart, *Employment and Earnings Inadequacy: A New Social Indicator* (Baltimore: Johns Hopkins University Press, 1974).

43. Ibid., p. 17.

44. William Spring, Bennett Harrison, and Thomas Vietorisz, "Crisis of the Underemployed," *New York Times Magazine*, November 5, 1972.

45. Herman P. Miller, "Subemployment in Poverty Areas of Large U.S. Cities," *Monthly Labor Review* 96 (October 1973):10–17.

46. Ibid., p. 10.

47. Sar A. Levitan and Robert B. Taggart, "Employment and Earnings Inadequacy: A Measure of Worker Welfare," *Monthly Labor Review* 96 (October 1973):19.

48. Thomas Vietorisz, Robert Mier, and Jean-Ellen Giblin, "Subemployment: Exclusion and Inadequacy Indexes," *Monthly Labor Review* 98 (May 1975):3–12.

49. Philip M. Hauser, "The Working Force in Developing Areas," in Ivar Berg (ed.), *Human Resources and Economic Welfare: Essays in Honor of Eli Ginzberg* (New York: Columbia University Press, 1972), pp. 141–161.

50. See Sullivan, *Marginal Workers, Marginal Jobs*.

51. Mayall and Nelson, *The Temporary Help Supply Service and the Temporary Labor Market*, p. 54.

52. Ruth Marlow, "Use temporaries, OPM Urges," *Federal Times* 20 (47) (1985):1 ff.

2. The Temporary Help Industry

1. National Association of Temporary Services, "The Temporary Help Service Industry" (Alexandria, Va.: National Association of Temporary Services, 1985, Brochure), p. 4.

2. Mitchell Fromstein, *The Socio-Economic Roles of the Temporary Help Service in the United States Labor Market*. (Washington, D.C.: GPO, 1977), pp. 16, 20.

3. Sar A. Levitan, Garth Mangum, and Ray Marshall, *Human Resources and Labor Markets*, 3d ed. (New York: Harper and Row, 1981).

4. Ibid., p. 473.

5. Kathy Berquist, Employers Overload, Minneapolis, Minn. October 8, 1985, Correspondence.

6. Telephone interview with Bruce Steinberg, NATS spokesperson, November 19, 1993.

7. National Association of Temporary Services, "Fact Sheet" (Alexandria, Va.: National Association of Temporary Services, various years).

8. Polly Callaghan and Heidi Hartmann, *Contingent Work: A Chartbook on Part-Time and Temporary Employment* (Washington, D.C.: Economic Policy Institute, 1991), p. 28.

9. Steven A. Wasser, "Economics of the Temporary Help Services Industry," *Contemporary Times* 3(9) (1984):15.

10. Ibid., p. 14.

11. Heidi Hartmann, and June Lapidus, "Temporary Work." (Washington, D.C.: Institute for Women's Policy Research, 1989), p. 4.

12. Callaghan and Hartmann, *Contingent Work*.

13. U.S. Department of Commerce, *1985 U.S. Industrial Outlook* (Washington, D.C.: GPO.

14. U.S. Department of Labor, "Employment, Hours, and Earnings, United States, 1981–93," Bureau of Labor Statistics Bulletin 2429 (Washington, D.C.: GPO, 1993), p. 431.

15. Callaghan and Hartmann, *Contingent Work*, p. 6.

16. Telephone interview with Steinberg.

17. National Association of Temporary Services, "Fact Sheet," (Alexandria, Va.: National Association of Temporary Services, 1990).

18. 9 to 5, National Association of Working Women, *Working at the Margins: Part-Time and Temporary Workers in the United States* (Cleveland: National Association of Working Women, 1986).

19. Telephone interview with Steinberg.

20. Ibid. See also Jane Applegate, "When the Economy Gets Tough, Smart Firms Get Temporary Workers," *Washington Post*, February 18, 1991.

21. Data from the Compact Disclosure electronic database, Bethesda, Maryland, September 1993.

22. Janice Castro, "Disposable Workers," *Time*, March 29, 1993, pp. 43–47.

23. "Survey of Austin Temporary Employment Services," *Austin Business Journal*, July 1–7, 1985, p. 14.

24. Christopher Sheehan, "Temporary Help Agencies Are Bullish on American Economy," *The Office* (March 1993):32 ff.

25. Laura Walbert, "Menpower Versus Penpower," *Forbes*, December 19, 1983, pp. 198–199.

26. "Parker Pen Unit to Set Up Clerical Agency in China," *Wall Street Journal*, September 5, 1984.

27. Joshua Mendes, "The Bright Side of the Mess at Manpower," *Fortune*, June 4, 1990, pp. 46–48.

28. "Teaching Office Skills," *IBM Innovation* (5) (1985):2–3.

29. Frank E. James, "Manpower, Inc. Seeks a Niche in High Tech," *Wall Street Journal*, February 6, 1984.

30. Ibid.

31. Ibid.

32. Cited in Kate Evans-Correria, "Office Temporaries," *Purchasing*, August 16, 1990, p. 97.

33. Jason Zweig, "Business Services and Supplies," *Forbes*, January 8, 1990, pp. 124–125.

34. Judith Berck, "Kelly Climbs from the '91 gloom," *New York Times*, April 26, 1992.

35. "The Corporate Elite," *Business Week*, October 19, 1990, p. 158.

36. Zweig, "Business Services and Supplies," p. 124.

37. "Kelly Donates Its Services to Nonprofit Groups," *Las Vegas Sun*, March 20, 1990.

38. Nancy Ten Kate, "Here Today Gone Tomorrow," *American Demographics* (December 1989):34–35.

39. Berck, "Kelly Climbs from the '91 Gloom."

40. Andy Zipser, "Employment Boom: Olsten Cashes in on Growing Demand for Temps," *Barron's*, July 13, 1992, p. 17.

41. Data from Compact Disclosure.

42. Ibid.

43. "Survey of Austin Temporary Employment Services," *Austin Business Journal*, July 1–7, 1985, p. 14.

44. National Association of Temporary Services, "The Temporary Help Service Industry" (Alexandria, Va.: National Association of Temporary Services, 1985, Mimeographed).

45. Advertisement for Eastridge Temps, *Las Vegas Review-Journal*, November 19, 1989.

46. Bob Whalen and Susan Dennis, "The Temporary Help Industry: An Annual Update," p. 2, reprint from *Contemporary Times* (Spring 1991).

47. Zweig, "Business Services and Supplies," p. 125.

48. Data from Compact Disclosure.

49. Mary Warner, "Providers of Home Healthcare Expand and Consolidate to Meet Rising Demand," Modern Healthcare, October 26, 1992, pp. 80–84.

50. Cited in Barbara Johnson, *Working Whenever You Want* (Englewood Cliffs, N.J.: Prentice-Hall, 1983), p. 134.

51. "Survey of Austin Temporary Employment Services," p. 14.

52. Friedman, Selma. 1982. "Temporary Help of the Specialized Kind," *Administrative Management* (April 1982):30.

53. Charles Grigsby, "Work," in Donald Bauman, Cheryl Beauvais, Charles Grigsby, and D. Franklin Schultz, "The Austin Homeless." (Austin: University of Texas, 1985, Mimeographed), pp. 117–144.

54. Heidi Gottfried, "Mechanisms of Control in the Temporary Help Service Industry," *Sociological Forum* (1991):699–713.

55. Cited in Joseph A. Litterer, *Organizations: Structure and Function* (New York: Wiley, 1969).

3. The Expansion of Contingent Labor Markets

1. Alfred L. Malabre, "U.S. Economy Excels at Generating Jobs," *Wall Street Journal*, April 9, 1984 sec. A.

2. George Silvestri and John Lukasiewicz, "Occupational Employment Projections," *Monthly Labor Review* 114 (November 1991):64–94.

3. Susan Helper, "Corporate Subcontracting," *Dollars and Sense* 139 (9) (1988):17.

4. Richard S. Belous, *The Contingent Economy: The Growth of the Temporary, Part-Time and Subcontracted Workforce*, (Washington, D.C.: National Planning Association, 1989).

5. U.S. Bureau of Labor Statistics, *Business Contracting-Out Practices*, Summary Report 87-8 (Washington, D.C.: GPO).

6. Belous, *The Contingent Economy*, p. 37.

7. Helper, "Corporate Subcontracting," p. 18.

8. "When Retirees Go Back on the Payroll," *Business Week*, November 22, 1982, pp. 112–116. see also Janet Mason, "The In-House Option," *Management World* (June 1982):13; Joan Bassett "Recruitment: Fidelity Investments Brings Temporary Employment In-House," *Personnel Journal* (December 1989):65–70; and Selwyn Feinstein, "Not Forgotten: More Companies Call Retirees Back for Temporary Work," *Wall Street Journal*, April 25, 1989.

9. "When Retirees Go Back on the Payroll," p. 112.

10. Mason, "The In-House Option," p. 13.

11. William Olsten, "The In-House Temp Option—Is It Really?" *Management World* (August 1982): 44.

12. Ibid., pp. 38, 44.

13. David A. Snow and Leon Anderson, *Down on Their Luck: A Study of Homeless Street People* (Berkeley and Los Angeles: University of California Press, 1993).

14. Charles Grigsby, 1985. "Work," in Donald J. Bauman, Cheryl Beauvaus, Charles Grigsby, and D. Franklin Schultz, "The Austin Homeless" (Austin: University of Texas, 1985, Mimiographed), pp. 117–144.

15. Lawrence Wickliffe and Robert E. Parker, "Labor Corners in Las Vegas: An Ethnographic Study" (Las Vegas: University of Nevada, Department of Sociology, 1991, Manuscript).

16. Ray Marshall, *Rural Workers in Rural Labor Markets* Salt Lake City: Olympus Research, 1974).

17. Cited in "New Harvest, Old Shame," PBS documentary aired April 17, 1990.

18. Leslie A. Whitener, "A Statistical Portrait of Hired Farmworkers," *Monthly Labor Review* 107 (June 1984):49.

19. Ibid., pp. 50–52.

20. Jennifer Dixon, "Migrant Farm Workers Facing Varied Abuses," *Las Vegas Review-Journal/Sun*, December 13, 1992.

21. Jim Carrier, "Migrant Laborers Take to Life on Road in Seasonal Harvests," *Austin American-Statesman* December 6, 1985, sec. D.

22. "New Harvest, Old Shame." See also "Migrant Workers' Life Span Concerns Health Officials," *Austin American-Statesman*, April 12, 1987; and Jack Jones, "Experts Study Plight of Migrant Workers in U.S." *Springfield News-Leader* (Missouri), September 28, 1987.

23. David Sedeno, "Migrant Workers, Residents Battle in California." *Las Vegas Review-Journal/Sun*, September 29, 1990.

24. "H-2 Worker," PBS documentary aired 1991.

25. Robert Pear, "Alien Laborers Due to Increase in Rule Revision," *Austin American-Statesman*, January 27, 1985.

26. Veta Christy, "Nuclear Janitors Risk Health and Safety," *Multinational Monitor* (February 1984): 6–7.

27. Mary Melville, *The Temporary Worker in the Nuclear Power Industry,* Monograph no. 1 (Worcester, Mass.: Clark University, Center for Technology, Environment, and Development, 1981), p. 6.

28. Ibid., p. 16.

29. Robert W. Kates and Bonnie Braine, "The Locus of Benefits and Risks of West Valley Wastes," in Roger E. Kasperson (ed.), *Equity Issues in Radioactive Waste Management* (Cambridge, Mass.: Oelgeschlager, Gunn and Hain, 1983), pp. 94–117.

30. Robert Gillette, " 'Transient' Nuclear Workers: A Special Case for Standards," *Science* 186 (415) (1974):125.

31. "On the Job at NFS," *Sierra Club Fact Sheet* (Buffalo) (August-September 1979).

32. Karl Z. Morgan, "Cancer and Low Level Ionizing Radiation," *Bulletin of the Atomic Scientists* 34 (7) (1978):38.

33. Much of the following material is from the excellent Southern Regional Council study *Hard Labor* (Atlanta: Southern Regional Council, 1988). This report presents an inside look at impermanent working arrangements.

34. Lyman Grant, "Lesson III: (Part-Time) for You and (Part-Time) for Me,/and (Part-Time) Yet for a Hundred Indecisions," *Texas Observer*, June 4, 1982.

35. Ibid.

36. Rochelle Lefkowitz, "Part-Time Profs Win Contract," *In These Times*, May 4–10, 1983, p. 7.

37. "Updates on AAUP Activities," *Footnotes* 14 (1) (Fall 1993):2.

38. Grant, "Lesson III."

39. Cassandra Knobloch, "Part-Time Instructor Characteristics," *Knackademics*, April 22, 1985, p. 3.

40. Ezra Bowen, "Academia's New Gypsies," *Time*, January 12, 1987, p. 65.

41. William Serrin, "Up to a Fifth of U.S. Workers Now Rely on Part-Time Jobs." *New York Times*, August 14, 1983 sec. A.

42. Kathleen Lathrop, "Temporaries Are a Way of Life on the Campus," *New York Times*, January 21, 1985.

43. Barbara L. Johnson, *Working Whenever You Want* (Englewood Cliffs, N.J.: Prentice-Hall, 1983).

44. Grant, "Lesson III," p. 11.

45. Office of Personnel Management, "New Authority to Make and Extend Temporary Limited Appointments" Federal Personnel Manual System Letter 316–21 (Washington, D.C.: GPO, 1985).

46. Ruth Marlow, "Use Temporaries, OPM Urges." *Federal Times* 20 (47) (1985):1 ff.

47. Office of Personnel Management, "New Use of Term Employment," Federal Personnel Manual System Letter 316–24 (Washington, D.C.: GPO, 1987), p. 1.

48. Office of the Federal Register, *Code of Federal Regulations 5: Parts 1 to 699* (Washington, D.C.: GPO, 1990), p. 126.

49. Donald Mayall and Kristin Nelson, *The Temporary Help Supply Service and the Temporary Labor Market* (Salt Lake City: Olympus Research 1982).

4. Temporary Clerical Workers

1. Bob Whalen and Susan Dennis, "The Temporary Help Industry: An Annual Update," pp. 1–4, reprint from *Contemporary Times* (Spring 1991).

2. Mitchell Fromstein, *The Socio-Economic Roles of the Temporary Help Service in the United States Labor Market.* (Washington, D.C.: GPO, 1977) pp. 16–17.

3. "Temporary Help to the Rescue!" *Modern Office Procedures* (May 1979):96.

4. Deborah Churchman, "High-Tech Training Gives 'Temps' New Professional Status," *Christian Science Monitor*, December 29, 1983.

5. Barbara Johnson, *Working Whenever You Want* (Englewood Cliffs, N.J.: Prentice-Hall, (1983), p. 7.

6. Martin J. Gannon, "Preferences of Temporary Workers: Time, Variety, and Flexibility," *Monthly Labor Review* 107 (August 1984):26–27.

7. Johnson, *Working Whenever You Want*, p. 8.

8. Ibid.

9. Donald Mayall and Kristin Nelson, *The Temporary Help Supply Service and the Temporary Labor Market* (Salt Lake City: Olympus Research 1982).

10. Kate Tomlin and Ron Kapche, speech to the Dallas Women's Network, July 21, 1984.

11. Teresia R. Ostrach, "A Second Look at Temporaries," *Personnel Journal* (June, 1981):441.

12. Howard Rudnitsky, "A Cushion for Business," *Forbes*, February 5, 1979, pp. 78–80.

13. Mike Kutka, "The Temporary—Becoming a Permanent Office Worker," *Management World* (September 1980):10.

14. "One Temporary Worker Speaks Out," *Contemporary Times* 4 (12A) (1985):26.

15. Johnson *Working Whenever You Want*, p. 34.

16. Ibid., p. 35.

17. Jamie Laughridge, "Temporary Work: How to Make It Work for You," *Harper's Bazaar* (April 1982): 236.

18. Tomlin and Kapche.

19. Sandra Roberts, "From Part-Time to Full-Time," *Black Enterprise* (July 1983):62.

20. Edward A. Lenz, "The Ties That Bind," *Contemporary Times* 4 (13) (1985):16.

21. "Why and How Business Uses Temporary Help," *The Office* (6) (1980):101.

22. Cited in "Temporary Help Now Is a Permanent Necessity," *The Office* (5) (1979):162.

23. Johnson, *Working Whenever You Want*, p. 28.

24. "Temporary Help Now Is a Permanent Necessity," p. 164.

25. Joseph McKendrick, "Temporary Help: Profile of a Growing Industry," *Management World* (June 1981):18.

26. "National Temporaries Week," *Temporary Topics* 1 (1) (1985):7.

27. Ibid.

28. Johnson, *Working Whenever You Want*, pp. 25–30.

29. Karen E. Debats, "Temporary Services Flourish," *Personnel Journal* (October, 1983):781–782.

30. Gannon, "Preferences of Temporary Workers," pp. 26–27.

31. 9 to 5, National Association of Working Women *Working at the Margins: Part-Time and Temporary Workers in the United States* (Cleveland: National Association of Working Women 1986).

5. Temporary Industrial Workers

1. Bob Whalen and Susan Dennis, "The Temporary Help Industry: An Annual Update," pp. 1–4, reprint from *Contemporary Times* (Spring 1991).

2. John M. Jermier, "Sabotage at Work: The Rational View," *Research in the Sociology of Organizations* 6 (1988):101–134.

3. Donald Mayall and Kristin Nelson, *The Temporary Help Supply Service and the Temporary Labor Market* (Salt Lake City: Olympus Research, 1982), p. 52.

6. The Growth of Contingent Work

1. Susan R. Sanderson and Lawrence Schein, "Sizing Up the Down-Sizing Era," *Across the Board* (November 1986):15–23.

2. "Flexible High-Flyers," *The Economist*, September 29, 1984, p. 71.

3. Anna Pollert, "The 'Flexible Firm': Fixation or Fact," *Work, Employment and Society* 2 (2) (1988):283.

4. Barry Bluestone and Bennett Harrison, *The Deindustrialization of America* (New York: Basic Books, 1982).

5. Daniel C. Struve, "Demand for Temporaries Spurs Opportunities," *The Office* (9) (1985):141.

6. Sam Sacco, "Temporary Help Industry: Its Impact on Business," *The Office* (9) (1985):38.

7. Cited in Ruth Walker, "Temporary-Help Industry, After Temporary Slack, Is Back Strong," *Christian Science Monitor*, July 30, 1984.

8. Cited in ibid.

9. "Behind Hiring of More Temporary Employees," *U.S. News and World Report*, February 25, 1985, p. 76.

10. Cited in David L. Farkas, "A Temporary Habit," *Modern Office Technology* (March 1985):94.

11. Walker, "Temporary-Help Industry, After Temporary Slack, Is Back Strong."

12. "Temporary Help Services—Who Uses Them and Why," *The Office* (5) (1984):129–133.

13. Heidi Gottfried, "Mechanisms of Control in the Temporary Help Service Industry," *Sociological Forum* 6 (4) (1991):699–713.

14. Richard C. Edwards, *Contested Terrain* (New York: Basic Books, 1979).

15. Camille Colatosti, "A Job Without a Future," *Dollars and Sense* (May 1992):9.

16. "Blue Shield, Struck, Plans to Shift Jobs," *San Francisco Examiner*, March 1, 1981.

17. Joseph McKendrick, "Temporary Help: Profile of a Growing Industry," *Management World* (June 1981):18.

18. "The Impact of Temporary Help on Productivity in Business," *The Office* (5) (1981):151.

19. Cited in Deborah Churchman, "High-Tech Training Gives 'Temps' New Professional Status," *Christian Science Monitor*, December 29, 1983.

20. Harry Braverman, *Labor and Monopoly Capital* (New York: Monthly Review Press, 1974).

INDEX

Adia Temporary Services, 109
American Association of University
    Professors, and part-time faculty,
    78

Babbage Principle of management,
    54
Belous, Richard, 1
Bluestone, Barry, 140
Braverman, Harry, 150–151
Bureau of Labor Statistics, 11, 14, 28,
    60
business cycle and temporary work,
    26

Canadian Federation of Temporary
    Help Services, 108
CDI Corporation, 40
Census Bureau, 10
clerical workers, *see* temporary cleri-
    cal workers
Commerce, U.S. Department of, 27
contingent work: defined, 1; expan-
    sion of, 57–83; future of, 41
contingent workers, 3–13, 57–83;
    defined, 1; wages of, 61
contingent workers, types of, 58;
    business service workers, 6–7; con-
    tract workers, 7–8, 58–61; day
    laborers, 3–5, 63–66; displaced
    workers, 13; farm workers, 66–68;
    federal workers, 18, 81–82; guest

workers, 5–6, 68–70; in-house tem-
    porary workers, 29, 61–62;
    involuntary part-time workers, 11–
    12; in the nuclear utility industry,
    70–73; part-time college faculty, 17,
    78–81; part-time workers, 10; tran-
    sient workers, 70; undocumented
    workers, 68; working poor (low-
    wage workers), 14
Cooperatively Organized and Run
    Employment Service, Inc. (CORE),
    75
corporate restructuring, 8, 138–139
Current Business Reports, 27

deindustrialization and temporary
    work, 140–145
deskilling, 150–151
Devine, Donald, 18
dual labor market theory, 15

economy, 13, 26, 137–140; peripheral
    and core sectors, 139–140
employee leasing, 41
Employers Overload, 25
Employment and Earnings Inadequa-
    cy Index, 16
employment growth, 27–28

farm operators, 5–6
financial deregulation, role of in con-
    tingent economy, 138–139